If a Chimpanzee Could Talk

and Other Reflections

on Language Acquisition

If a Chimpanzee Could Talk

and Other Reflections

on Language Acquisition

Jerry H. Gill

The University of Arizona Press ⋅ Tucson

The University of Arizona Press

© 1997 Arizona Board of Regents

All rights reserved

⊗ This book is printed on acid-free, archival-
quality paper.

Manufactured in the United States of America

02 01 00 99 98 97   6 5 4 3 2 1

Library of Congress Cataloging-in-Publication Data

Gill, Jerry H.
If a chimpanzee could talk and other reflections on
language acquisition / Jerry H. Gill.
   p.   cm.
Includes bibliographical references and index.
ISBN 0 – 8165 – 1668 – 5 (cloth : acid-free paper).
ISBN 0 – 8165 – 1669 – 3 (paper : acid-free paper)
1. Language acquisition.   2. Language and culture.
I. Title.
P118.G53   1997
401′.93 — dc20   96-25306
CIP

British Library Cataloguing-in-Publication Data

A catalogue record for this book is available from the
British Library.

For Ian

Contents

Preface

The phenomenon of first-language acquisition has held a special fascination for me ever since I first saw the play *The Miracle Worker* in 1963. Over the years I have followed up nearly every opportunity to gather more information about and explore the implications of instances of beings, human or otherwise, who seem to exist on the threshold between speech and not-quite-speech. Not surprisingly, this interest ran parallel to and even intersected with my philosophical concern with the nature of language and meaning. About ten years ago I began putting my reflections into written form, focusing on specific cases, such as Helen Keller, "wolf" children, and chimpanzees. This book comprises the results of my efforts thus far, a kind of "mid-project report."

I am deeply indebted to the editorial staff of the University of Arizona Press for undertaking the publication of this book, since it is the kind of topic that generally falls between traditional disciplinary categories and thus never sees the light of day. Also, I wish to thank my typist, Dorothyanne Peltz, for her enthusiasm for and competence in turning my rather patchwork collection into a real manuscript.

Finally, I take this opportunity to express once more my deep appreciation to my wife, Mari Sorri, for her never-ending encouragement, interest, and criticism. Having a colleague for a life companion is surely one of life's greatest gifts, especially when she knows how to laugh!

If a Chimpanzee Could Talk

and Other Reflections

on Language Acquisition

Introduction:

The Why and Wherefore

The acquisition of natural language has always puzzled me. Indeed, the more I have thought about the various aspects of this process, the more mysterious it seems. Over the years I have read numerous books and articles on the subject, yet even though they all have been enlightening in one way or another, they all raise and leave unanswered additional questions and paradoxes. Perhaps the most amazing fact about all natural languages is that none are in any sense more "primitive" than others. That is to say, none of the thousands of natural languages so far encountered are of the "Me-Tarzan-you-Jane" variety. Even the Stone Age Aborigines of the Australian "outback" speak highly complex and distinctive languages. As anthropologists put it, there simply is no evidence that language, as a universal human phenomenon, has evolved from simple, more basic versions into richer, more sophisticated varieties. Language, in all its complexity and fullness, seems already to have been on hand whenever and wherever human beings were born.

It is, to be sure, possible to infer — and rational theorizing would seem to require it — that language initially might, indeed must, have developed out of the various experiences, gestures, and vocalizations of proto human beings. Yet there is absolutely no indication of such development within the languages of even the most "basic" cultures or tribal peoples so far discovered. The simple fact is that fully developed language lies at the very heart of all human experience and culture. Wherever and whenever there have been peoples in any way resembling those we know as human beings, there have been highly complex and rich natural languages. Indeed, it is not going too far to say that it is incorporation into a speaking community that constitutes becoming a human being. For among humans, unlike other less complex animal forms, nearly all behavior is learned rather than

3

instinctive, and it is through language that both individual and cultural experience are learned.

The acquisition of natural language is no less puzzling when one focuses on the experience of the individual person. Over the years I have observed rather carefully my own children's enculturation in and through speech in an effort to pinpoint the threshold or crucial stages involved. This enterprise has been singularly unrewarding. Although I have learned a great deal and enjoyed the process very much, the mystery of language acquisition remains. Children move from random oral-play through responsive interaction and imitation to one-word declarations and simple conversations in a matter of eighteen to twenty months. Moreover, they accomplish this in an almost imperceptible manner, sliding from one stage to the next piecemeal and unpredictably. Natural speech is an emergent phenomenon, with each stage evolving from the previous without being deducible from it. When my children were about a year old, it seemed that they would never to be able to talk, and yet one year later invariably we engaged in significant, albeit simple, conversations.

One of the fundamental errors one can make when considering the acquisition of natural language is to assume that it is similar to that of acquiring a second or nonnatural language. This is an understandable mistake, but one that many who should know better, especially philosophers of language, continue to make. The logical gap between (1) moving from one's natural language to another language and (2) coming into one's natural language from none at all is like that between moving from square one to square two and getting to square one in the first place. The former is moving within the game, while the latter is entering into the game or getting to square one from what might be called "square zero." In short, it would seem that in order to acquire language one must already have it. Thus it seems that language is logically impossible. The mystery remains.

A different but equally fatal mistake is that of assuming that at the fundamental level all speech is learned by means of pointing, or what philosophers call "ostensive definition." The names or primary qualities of various objects or persons are often taught by pointing to or even touching them. However, not only does this not explain how more abstract concepts or absent objects are defined, but it fails even to broach the question of how pointing itself is learned. For pointing is a kind of linguistic sign in its own right; indeed, it might even be described as the key or most basic signifier of all. But it, too, must initially be learned, and this acquisition cannot also be based on pointing; it cannot, it seems, presuppose itself. In fact, it would seem that ostensive definition, rather than explaining how natural language is acquired, only intensifies the mystery. Once again, it appears that in order to learn how to understand the meaning of pointing, one must already know it.

Following up on my continuing puzzlement over language has led me, over the years, to study and write about a number of different aspects of the phenomenon of speech in which the question of the threshold between meaningful linguistic activity and instinctive or merely conditioned behavior arises. Since this threshold is the concern of linguists, literary theorists, anthropologists, psychologists, and philosophers alike, my investigations have necessarily been interdisciplinary in nature. The essays comprising the present book represent the different angles of approach as well as the diverse fields of study that can be involved in pursuing the paradoxes of language acquisition. Admittedly, my own particular interests are more philosophical than scientific, and the topics of concern in the following chapters clearly reflect this proclivity. At the same time, however, I have sought to explore and employ the insights of those working in related fields in a responsible and fruitful manner.

The chapters have been arranged according to a continuum ranging from one side of the threshold of language to the other. Thus we begin by considering whether and how chimpanzees might be said to engage in language and finish with questions arising from cross-cultural translation and interpretation. Along the way the phenomena of "wolf children," Helen Keller, and normal language acquisition are also examined. The book concludes with some general reflections and suggestions concerning the overall significance of these various topics and explorations for the philosophy of language. However, I have made no attempt to explain the mystery of the threshold of language. Rather, my intention throughout the chapters, as well as in the conclusion, is to allow the diverse facets and dynamics of this phenomenon to display themselves, even if they cannot be straightforwardly stated. As Emily Dickinson knew, deep truth can only be expressed indirectly, "on the slant," as it were.

For these reasons the following chapters do not combine to present anything like a step-by-step argument or a well-focused conclusion. Rather, each comes at the central topic from a different, somewhat oblique angle seeking to explore and reveal the puzzle of the threshold of language without "solving" it. Chapter 1 examines the work of a number of psychologists who have spent many years in an effort to teach sign language to chimpanzees. Not only do their efforts cast considerable light on the relationship between linguistic activity and the definition of human nature, but they focus a number of philosophical issues concerning the meaning of meaning itself. Chapter 2 examines the studies of children who have spent a considerable part of their childhood outside the human linguistic community. The comparison and contrast that can be made between such children and the chimpanzees discussed in the first chapter are especially interesting and instructive.

Chapter 3 takes up various attempts on the part of quite diverse philosophers to understand the threshold of language as it surfaced in Helen Keller's initiation into a fully human and cognitive life by means of sign language. Keller's experience and accomplishment, together with her own accounts of them, may offer the closest thing available to a "laboratory experiment" involving the successful acquisition of language. Once again, the similarities and differences between and among Keller, the various "wolf children," and the chimpanzees are fascinating and significant. Her linguistic success, in contrast to the near total failure of the feral children, even though they possessed essentially the same genetic endowment, stands out as strongly as her ability to outdistance the minimally successful chimpanzees. She achieved in a month what the chimpanzees needed years and even "normal" children take many months to accomplish. Moreover, Keller went on to linguistic levels far beyond those of most human adults.

Chapter 4 explores the methodology, along with its implications for the philosophy of language, employed by Barry and Samahria Kaufman in retrieving their son Raun from autism. Although a number of experts diagnosed Raun very early as suffering from severe autism, he was "cured" by his parents' efforts to reach him, not by insisting that he come out of his private, inner world into theirs but by seeking to enter his world through imitating his idiosyncratic behavior patterns. Raun acquired language and developed into a normal child not by imitating the adults around him but by having them establish contact with him through imitating and affirming him. Thus the nature of imitation in language acquisition turns out to be a two way street involving reciprocal interaction between speakers and learners.

Chapter 5 seeks to present and evaluate the findings of a large number of psycholinguists who have been studying various aspects of language acquisition for several decades. In spite of the obvious interest and value inherent within these studies, upon closer inspection nearly all of them assume that linguistic cognition is essentially, if not entirely, a matter of mental processes and procedures. The role of bodily and social activity is systematically excluded from studies that begin by defining knowledge in terms of mental "mechanisms," "inferences," and "hypotheses." Such processes emerge from linguistic skills, not vice versa.

Chapter 6 seeks to examine many of the previous issues as they arise in the context of cross-cultural understanding, with specific reference to linguistic translation and interpretation. The case in point is the confusion and political manipulation that resulted from the failure of early immigrants to the Americas to take Native American cultures and languages seriously. Their assumption that these diverse, complex, and indigenous cultures and languages were "primitive," minimal, and essentially the same led the transplanted Europeans to the conclusion that there existed a barrier, not simply a threshold, between themselves and the Indians. Specifically, it was assumed that the native peoples spoke a simple "Dick-and-Jane" code that relied heavily on sign language. Thus their adult cognitive capacities were thought to correspond to those of white children. The discussion of the concrete particulars involved in these issues contributes to an understanding of the threshold of language.

Chapter 7 takes up the significance of the work of Benjamin Lee Whorf for our understanding of the relationship between the structure of a natural language and the patterns of thought of its speakers. Following the initial suggestions of Edward Sapir, Whorf claimed that the structure of Indo-European languages is markedly different from that of Native American languages, and that this difference reflects an important difference in the ways the respective speakers arrange their worlds conceptually and pragmatically. The chapter analyzes many of Whorf's examples and inferences with an eye to their implications for the idea that reality is in fact linguistically constituted.

Finally, in the concluding chapter, a summation of major issues factoring into the discussions of the previous chapters is offered, together with some general reflections on character and place of language in relation to human nature and culture. More pointedly, specific conclusions are drawn concerning the implications of these investigations for the philosophy of language. These implications are found to dovetail nicely with the insights of various philosophers, including Ludwig Wittgenstein, J. L. Austin, Maurice Merleau-Ponty, Michael Polanyi, Owen Barfield, and Nelson Goodman. Once again, however, it should be borne in mind that both the aim and the claim of this entire study is not the full explication of the threshold of language but, rather, the revealing of its contours and dynamics. The degree of its overall significance should be, by means of this process, better able to speak for itself. It is hoped that these reflections will provide a useful point of departure for yet further explorations of the linguistic threshold.

1

If a Chimpanzee Could Talk

The title of this chapter is an extrapolation from Ludwig Wittgenstein's remark "If a lion could talk, we could not understand him" (*Philosophical Investigations*, p. 223). The point of that remark was to call attention to the fact that linguistic meaning is woven into the very fabric of the human-way-of-being in the world, into what Wittgenstein called "the human form of life." Since lions do not participate in this form of life, we presumably would not know how to take or what to do with their utterances.

The aim of the present chapter is to explore the philosophical ramifications of certain extensive and provocative efforts to teach sign language to chimpanzees. These efforts are documented in the fascinating book *Teaching Sign Language to Chimpanzees* by R. A. and B. T. Gardner. To date, little if any attention has been paid by philosophers to the facts and implications of this endeavor for questions about the nature of language in general and the notion of meaning in particular.

The Structure of the Study

In 1966 the Gardners began their experimental investigations with a ten-month-old chimpanzee named Washoe under auspices of the psychology department at the University of Nevada, Reno. Their goal was to discover whether and to what degree a chimpanzee could learn American Sign Language (ASL). Because the chimpanzee's genetic and anatomical structure, as well as physical and social behavior, is closest to that of human beings, the assumption was that this might well be a possibility.

The Gardners chose to raise and teach Washoe within the context of their own home and family life, a method they term "cross-fostering," rather than within that of the operant conditioning laboratory. In short, they sought to replicate, as far as possible, the context and process of a human child acquiring its natural language. More specifically, their goal was to raise and teach Washoe in essentially the same way as deaf foster parents would raise a deaf child. Thus the only language they used in her presence was ASL. Over a period of about four years Washoe learned to distinguish and use effectively over 130 signs.

> She asked for goods and services, and she also asked questions about the world of objects and events around her. When Washoe had about eight signs in her expressive vocabulary, she began to combine them into meaningful phrases. YOU ME HIDE, and YOU ME GO OUT HURRY were common. . . . Along with her skill with cups and spoons, and pencils and crayons, her signing developed stage for stage much like the speaking and signing of human children. (p. 6)

It is important to bear in mind that ASL is not a kind of semaphore or Morse code for English. Rather, it is the bona fide natural language of deaf people of North America, comprising its own vocabulary and grammatical structure, much of which is communicated through the inflections of modulated gestures and facial expressions.

In 1970 Washoe went to live at the University of Oklahoma, in Norman, with Professor Roger Fouts. Two years later the Gardners began a more ambitious project. Between 1972 and 1976 they acquired four additional chimpanzees (Moja, Pili, Tatu, and Dar) and set out to replicate their work with Washoe in relation to a set of cross-fostered siblings. As Jane Goodall has clearly established, chimpanzees are extremely social, especially within the bonds of family, with siblings playing an important role in teaching one another. The Gardners hoped that this pattern would facilitate and enhance the goals of the project. Their hopes were, indeed, fulfilled. This "extended family" was moved to a guest ranch on the outskirts of Reno.

The two main techniques employed in teaching the young chimpanzees sign language were modeling and molding. The former involves the process of operant conditioning, whereby the learner's natural and/or random behavior is consistently rewarded whenever the desired pattern is performed. Although this method is useful in certain cases, especially at the beginning stages, it turned out to be too slow and inefficient for rapid and extensive development. Molding, on the other hand, involves molding the hands of the learner into the desired sign while putting them through the appropriate movements. This technique is used in teaching all sorts of motor skills to humans, both children and adults, as well. The backdrop for these specific methods was constant linguistic and behavioral interaction.

The results of this second experiment were every bit as significant as those of the first. In the Gardners' own words:

> Washoe, Moja, Pili, Tatu, and Dar signed to friends and to strangers. They signed to each other and to themselves, to dogs and to cats, toys, tools, even to trees. . . . They also used the elementary sorts of sign language inflections that deaf children use to modulate the meaning of signs. . . . Cross-fostered chimpanzees converse among themselves, even when there is no human being present and the conversations must be recorded with remotely controlled cameras. (p. 24)

Six years after relocating with Professor Fouts in Oklahoma, Washoe was given an "adopted" son, Loulis. At this juncture an entirely new and crucial phase of the ongoing experiment was introduced. In order to determine whether or not communication through sign language can be acquired without human intervention, all human signing was eliminated when Loulis was present. Later Washoe's Nevada "family" joined her and Loulis in Oklahoma, thus greatly facilitating Loulis's acquisition of language entirely apart from human input. Here again the results were nothing short of dramatic. Not only did Loulis learn sign language, but the learning was reciprocal.

> To show that Loulis could learn signs from chimpanzees, human beings did not use ASL signs in his presence (with the exception of seven question signs, WHO, WHAT, WHERE, WHICH, WANT, SIGN and NAME). Instead, Fouts and his associates used vocal English and the rich repertoire of human and chimpanzee nonverbal gestures, postures, and calls to interact with Washoe and Loulis. When Washoe signed to them, they responded appropriately; for example, if she signed DRINK, she was given a drink, or told, in English, that she would get a drink in a little while. If anyone erred and signed when Loulis was present, the instance was recorded. Over the five years of the experiment, there were fewer than 40 such instances. (p. 282)

In the early 1980s Professor Fouts moved the entire chimpanzee "family" to Central Washington State University in Ellensburg, Washington, where the experiment continued. In 1986, seven years into this phase of the project, the policy of having no human signers in Loulis's presence was rescinded. By this time he had acquired from Washoe and his other "siblings" nearly seventy signs, which he recognized and employed on an everyday basis. Although the project is still underway, it is apparent that the speed and quantity of the chimpanzees' acquisition of sign language are considerably less than that of humans.

Nevertheless, the learning and meaningful use of sign language by the chimpanzees has far exceeded what many had thought possible. Moreover, it raises extremely interesting and important issues not only for the philosophy of language but for psychology and anthropology as well. In his conclusion to the Gardners' volume, William C. Stokoe, of the Linguistics Department at Gallaudet College for the Deaf in Washington, D.C., wrote:

> These well-documented facts force a reconsideration of theory. The chimpanzees by definition can have no human language organ, and therefore their use of sign language signs in context and appropriately must result from the cognitive abilities of the chimpanzee plus consistent interaction with a human being using a linguistic system in the visual-gestural mode. The possibility then arises that there is a continuum in nature — even primate nature; what the human infant also experiences between birth and later childhood may result from human (and primate) cognitive abilities plus interaction with others, and not from a genetic "black box." (p. 315)

The Results of the Study

An obvious but nonetheless significant feature of the teaching of sign language to chimpanzees is its basis in natural gestures (p. 16). Although chimpanzees, whether wild or domesticated, are far less active vocally than humans, they are extremely active with their hands. Just as human languages arise out of natural human sounds, so the signs of ASL are made with natural human hand movements. Thus, these chimpanzees learned to imitate the human gestures employed in signing quite easily. Moreover, the gestures involved in this process are closely tied to various forms of natural behavior, such as touching, eating, smelling, and the like. They can be said to arise from a kind of "somatic onomatopoeia" paralleling that underlying much-spoken language. Indeed, the chimpanzees were far more "vocal" with their hand signs than they were with oral expression. Their voice activity remained about the same as that of chimpanzees in the wild (p. 50).

The researchers working with Loulis, Professors Deborah and Roger Fouts in Oklahoma, found that gestures developed into signs gradually. They give the following account of Loulis's acquisition of "come" and/or "gimme":

In early COME/GIMMEs, Loulis extended his arm in front of himself, palm up, for one to three seconds. In the following months, the form of sign improved as Loulis began to flex the extended hand. He also began to babble or play with this sign, making it in a variety of unrelated contexts. By August, 1980, he was using COME/GIMME almost entirely in appropriate contexts, and at this time, his nonverbal behavior started to complement the COME/GIMME signs. For example, when offered a highly preferred food or drink, Loulis now looked directly at the object while he food-grunted and signed GIMME. He began to orient the sign toward humans or chimpanzees, and he gazed at the face of the addressee. During the second meeting of Loulis and Moja, when the connecting cage door was opened, Loulis oriented toward Moja and signed COME directly to her. Moja approached the signing infant, and initiated a play interaction. COME/GIMME became a distinct sign for Loulis, quite separate from reaching or the natural chimpanzee begging gesture. In approximately 25% of the COME/GIMME signs that Loulis made, he used one hand to sign and the other hand to reach or to make the begging gesture. (p. 284)

Language acquisition arises from a combination of imitation and invention (p. 19). This interactive process was the very axis of the chimpanzees' learning of sign language. For example, the sign for "dog" is made by patting the thigh with an open hand. When Moja was twenty-four months old, she learned to make this sign on a human friend's thigh in order to get him to bark and go down on all fours like a dog. When Pili was sixteen months old, his use of the sign for dog was minimal until he learned this "dog game" from Moja. After only one instance of watching Moja play it with a mutual friend, the game became a favorite game of his also and his use of the sign greatly increased.

This creative adaptation of various signs can also be seen in the chimpanzees' invention of novel name combinations of their own

(p. 81). For instance, Washoe consistently referred to the refrigerator by signing "open food drink," even though her human companions called it the "cold box." Likewise, she referred to her toilet as "dirty good" instead of more conventional "potty chair." Other examples of this sort of "poetic license" can be found in the chimpanzees use of "metal hot" for a cigarette lighter, "listen drink" for a glass of Alka-Seltzer, "water bird" for ducks, as well as "cry hurt food" and "candy drink" for previously unnamed radishes and watermelon, respectively.

Perhaps the most interesting case of this creative modulation of signs was Washoe's alteration of the name of one human companion's name (p. 285). Because he had long hair, this person's name had been signed by moving the open hand down the back of the head. In order to gain this person's attention when his back was turned, Washoe modified his name by slapping the top of her head, thus making the sign audible. This adaptation worked so well that it evolved into Washoe's general attention-getting sign for anyone who was not looking at her. Her teachers designated this the "person" or "Hey you" sign, and the younger chimpanzees all learned this sign from Washoe and used it in the same way.

The success of this project seems to have been largely a function of the fact that it took place in an environment modeled after the living and learning conditions of a human household rather than after that of an operant conditioning laboratory (p. 23). The latter environment was tried at Columbia University, and not only were the results minimal, but the process became fundamentally counterproductive because the reward system short-circuited the potential for actual and reciprocal communication. Training, rather than learning, was the only positive outcome. The various phases of the Washoe project all resulted in the chimpanzees acquiring and using signs across a wide variety of contexts and task-oriented situations because the learning took place in an environment full of people, other chimpanzees, household and natural objects, shared activities, and pervasive, interactive communication.

It should also be noted in this connection that the various experimenters constituting the "family" of the chimpanzees were all trained to be able to identify and imitate the main chimpanzee vocalizations, notably pant-hoots, rough-grunts, laughter, whimpers, and screams.

This training greatly facilitated the natural interaction between the human teachers and chimpanzees, thus fostering the dynamic reciprocity so crucial in the acquisition of language. The training also enabled the experimenters to read the behavior context of various chimpanzee signings and thereby more accurately interpret their meanings. The natural, family household setting of this entire project made this training as easy as it was necessary.

Another indication of the significance of the different contexts in these two experiments is the fact that Nim, one of the chimpanzees who actually worked in both environments, showed far greater facility for vocabulary acquisition and conversational participation when moved from the operant condition training laboratory to the type of "family" context provided by the Washoe project. The findings of two independent researchers confirm this:

> The conversational analysis revealed that a high percentage of Nim's utterances were repetitious of his interlocutors' prior utterances and that his spontaneous contributions were extremely rare. Such a pattern of conversational interaction cast doubt on the achievements of all signing chimpanzees. It presented a picture of chimpanzees simply "aping" signs, and perhaps performing other tricks of the hand for rewards. Yet the entire corpus on which this conclusion was based consisted of training and testing situations. No relaxed conversational interactions were included. Our conversational sample indicated that Nim's conversational behavior under such conditions does not reflect his entire repertoire. The evidence presented here demonstrates that Nim's conversational behavior in a relaxed conversational social interaction was very different from his behavior in a training or testing situation. We question whether conclusions about conversational skills can be drawn from an analysis of interactions that are more didactic than sociable. (p. 276)

Washoe came to regularly sign to herself in private, when playing and looking at magazines, and even engaged in self-correction.

> Washoe, Moja, Pili, Tatu, and Dar both learned and used the signs of ASL in an environment modelled after the living and learning conditions of a human household. We did not have to tempt them with threats or ply them with questions to get them to sign to us. They initiated conversations on their own, and they commonly named objects and pictures of objects in situations in which we were unlikely to reward them. (p. 23)

Sometimes, when she was moving through a forbidden area, the videorecorder caught her signing "quiet," and when running to her potty chair she signed "hurry." On one occasion, when looking at an advertisement, she signed "food," studied her hand (not the picture), and changed her sign to "drink," which was correct. Such behavior clearly indicates that Washoe's learning was not limited to specific contexts and/or reinforcements. Rather, it was a task and communication oriented, just like that of human children.

This mention of behavior context gives rise to yet another distinctive feature of this project, namely, the chimpanzee's use of pragmatic devices, such as reiteration, as a means of modulating the meaning of their signing. The Gardners point out that until recently such devices were ignored even in the study of language acquisition among human children. The assumption appears to have been that since reiterations are redundant informationally, they can be edited out of the transcripts of children's speech development. Fortunately, this tendency is now being reversed, since even slight modulations in tone, stress, and facial expression, as well as repetition of a term or statement, can greatly alter the meaning of any utterance.

To be more specific, reiterations among both speaking children and signing chimpanzees are most clearly associated with answers to questions and announcements. Emphasis or assent is generally indicated by repeating the answer. "When, for example, Tatu was asked 'who you?' she replied 'Tatu Tatu'" (p. 211). This same principle applies when part of the question is incorporated into the answer. "When Moja was asked 'where grapes?' she replied, 'Grapes there'" (p. 210). Even when the chimpanzees answered incorrectly, such devices serve to indicate the vectorial character and categorical range of their linguistic behavior.

The learning of indexical and demonstrative signs is as crucial for chimpanzees as it is for humans. The sign "me" is an extended index finger pointed to the signer's chest, while the sign "you" is an index finger pointed at the addressee's chest. "This," "that," "here," and "there" are signed by pointing in the appropriate direction with the index finger. Such ostensive definitions, like the significance of pointing itself, are very difficult to learn because they are neither proper names, qualities, nor categories. Although it seems likely that the meaning of such indexes and demonstratives is derived from the act of pointing, it is not clear how the significance of pointing is grasped in the first place, since one cannot define it ostensively.

It seems highly probable that pointing itself is initially derived from touching and might be said to function as a kind of "touching at a distance." Indeed, in studies of both human and chimpanzee signers, it is common to observe what is referred to as "baby sign" (baby talk), in which both parents and children actually form simple signs on the body of the addressee. Deaf human parents frequently make their signs on their infants and vice versa, just as the Gardners and their cross-fostered chimpanzees did to each other. In addition to being an excellent way to get the child's attention, such "baby sign" serves as expression of approval or playfulness. Deaf couples even use each other's bodies for sign placing in lovemaking (p. 241).

In another instance, the experimenters had been employing the sign "napkin" to refer to Washoe's bib, as well as to table napkins. One evening just before dinner, Washoe's bib was held up and she was asked "what this?" whereupon she immediately signed "please gimme, please gimme gimme." Then with her two index finders she drew the outline of a bib on her chest, without using the sign for napkin. Although the experimenters remarked that this was a better sign for bib, since it was more precise than napkin, they decided against using it because "human children have to learn the language they find in the adult community, and so should a properly cross-fostered chimpanzee" (p. 61).

However, when they presented their Washoe project to the faculty and students at the California School for the Deaf in Berkeley a few months later, the experimenters were informed that the standard ASL sign for bib was made exactly the way Washoe had invented the sign for herself (p. 61). What the Gardners had overlooked was the simple fact that children frequently introduce new words, derived from various natural sounds or mistaken pronunciations, into their family's vocabulary. My own one-year-old did this with the sound of "bluh," which was her version of the word "blow," which we used to warn her that the cereal was hot. Soon she, and eventually we with her, was referring to cereal as "bluh." This term even found its way into our weekly shopping list.

Although the vast majority of the instances of chimpanzees using sign language reported in the Gardners' book are ones in which the chimpanzees are answering questions put to them by experimenters, there are several examples of a different, more extreme nature. These are the instances of spontaneous utterances on the part of the chimpanzees; indeed, the Gardners claim that spontaneous utterances outnumber elicited responses quite significantly (p. 63). One extremely provocative case occurred when Dar signed "bird" while gazing out the window, although his human companion failed to see any bird. Perhaps his companion had just missed seeing the bird, or perhaps Dar had mistaken a blowing leaf for a bird. Perhaps, however, Dar was expressing an associational relationship or even an expectation or wish with respect to the window and seeing birds (p. 64).

A similar example occurred when Washoe signed "dog" when the family was driving past a fence where a dog usually barked at their car, even though this time the dog did not appear. It is not clear whether Washoe was simply noting the usual association or actually commenting on the dog's absence—or even expressing relief with respect to the latter (p. 64). Further study of such spontaneous utterances is needed in order to explore the range and depth of meaning of the chimpanzee's use of sign language.

At the other extreme are those situations in which a response had to be coaxed out of one of the chimpanzees. The Gardners had a great deal of difficulty getting Washoe to use the sign "no." They tried giving her unreasonable demands, like ordering her to bed in the middle of the afternoon, but this failed because either she was generally good-natured enough to go along with these demands or she could get by without saying anything. Eventually they began to make up stories about there being a big mean dog outside, for example, and then asking Washoe if she wished to go outdoors. This stratagem generally produced the desired "no" (p. 65).

In the context of discussing the chimpanzees' occasional placing of their signs on the body of the addressee, the Gardners report that frequently certain facial expressions and/or sounds became correlated with various signs in the chimpanzees' ASL vocabulary. For example, a kissing sound came to be associated with the signing of "good" and "kiss," a sniffing sound with the signing of "funny" and "flower," and exhalations with "yes" and "who." Likewise, protruding lips went with "blow" and "who." In some cases the chimpanzees moved their heads as well as their hands in certain patterns, even though no ASL signs, except "yes" and "no," involve head movements.

It became a regular practice for the experimenters to rely on the chimpanzees for information about the daily goings-on in their common environment. For instance, Washoe would frequently and correctly "announce" who was entering or leaving the compound from her superior vantage point high up in her favorite tree. Once when she had lost a toy down a hole in the inner wall of her trailer, she got Professor Gardner's attention by signing "open, open" many times over the area just beneath the hole. There was a shared sense of excitement when the toy was retrieved from within the wall. It was perfectly clear that fresh information, true communication, not mere operant conditioning, had been exchanged in the resolution in this minor crisis.

One of the more interesting aspects of this project concerns the process of the chimpanzees learning that signs other than proper names are, in fact, not proper names but signs that indicate broad categories or sets. The Gardners guarded against unintentional "cuing" on the part of the testers by using slides of natural objects, which could be seen only by the chimpanzees but the order of which could be checked after the training session had been run. In addition, each slide was shown to the subject chimpanzee only once, and only a few examples of each type of object were introduced. As the Gardners explain it:

> Early in Project Washoe we worried that the signs might become too closely associated with their initial referents. It turned out that this was no more a problem for Washoe or any of our other subjects than it is for children. The chimpanzees easily transferred the signs they had learned for a few balls, shoes, flowers, or cats to the full range of categories whenever they found them and however represented, as if they divided the world into the same conceptual categories that human beings use. (p. 193)

Crucial to all language acquisition is the comprehension of the meaning of the "wh-" questions: who, what, where, when, and why. In addition to asking for information about the world, these questions indicate the sort of information being asked for. All of the chimpanzees in the different phases of this project showed, even in their semantic mistakes, that they understood the logical function of "wh-" questions. Moreover, as we have already seen, they frequently repeated or incorporated the signs for these questions into their answers. It is never made clear, however, whether or not the chimpanzees ever asked or answered "why" and "when" questions. Giving and asking for reasons and locations in time are presumably more complex activities than those involved in the other "wh-" questions.

Although English relies heavily on word order for the modulation of meaning in relation to any given utterance, ASL, like many human languages, relies more on inflectional devices such as doubling. For instance, the sign for "like" is done with two hands for emphasis to show that one likes something very much, while the sign for "eat," when made with both hands alternately and repeatedly, indicates a big meal or banquet. In addition, a number of interactive verbs, such as "ask," "give," and "meet," make use of the vectorial "sight-line" as a substitute for the personal pronouns "me" and "you." Moreover, reiteration can serve to change "house" into "town," "tree" into "forest," "sit" into "chair," "fly" into "airplane," and even to render "hope" emphatic (pp. 240 – 41).

Earlier it was mentioned how the modulation of meaning can be effected through the use of "baby sign," that is, by the signer placing signs on the various parts of the addressee's body. For example, "tickle" and "swallow" are normally signed on the back of one's own hand and on one's own throat, respectively. The Gardners report that the chimpanzees frequently made such signs on the corresponding part of the addressee's body. The following report of such modulation is typical: "Greg was hooting and making other sounds, to prevent Dar from falling asleep. Dar put his fist to Greg's lips and made kissing sounds. Greg asked, WHAT WANT? and Dar replied, QUIET, placing the sign on Greg's lips (GRG 5/19/81)" (p. 243). A different report is similar: "After Dar eats his breakfast cereal, I feed him banana. Dar signs with his hands under the table. I tell Dar, CAN'T SEE and then Dar signs SEE BANANA, making the BANANA sign over his head (VC 7/7/79)" (p. 243).

Three especially significant developments occurred in the area of meaning modulation. The first was when the chimpanzees would actually take the addressee's hand and mold it into the sign they themselves wished to express: "After her nap, Washoe signed OUT.

I was hoping for Washoe to potty herself and did not comply. Then Washoe took my hands and put them together to make OUT, and then signed OUT with her own hands, to show me how. Again today, Washoe signed UP and then took my hand and signed UP with it (NR 11/15/87)" (p. 234 – 44). The second occurred when the chimpanzees showed perplexity and then elation when unexpected behavior was encountered and then overcome: "Moja signed DOG on Ron and me, and looked at our faces, waiting for us to 'woof.' After several rounds, I made a 'meeow' instead. Moja signed DOG again. I repeated 'meeow' again, and Moja slapped my leg harder. This went on. Finally I woofed and Moja leapt on me and hugged me (TT 1/4/75)" (p. 244). The third development was when the chimpanzees employed the "questioning look," which is the ASL equivalent of the rising pitch that distinguishes questions from statements in English: "Tatu takes a picture book and looks through it. I join her. Seems to be especially interested in pictures of flowers and of chimpanzees. Tatu points to flowers, THERE?, with raised eyebrows and prolonged eye contact. I sign FLOWER then Tatu turns back to another page (KW 12/23/76)" (p. 244). All of these behaviors embody qualities that clearly characterize the intangible aspects comprised by human linguistic activity. The videorecords of these incidents and many others like them constitute an extremely provocative phenomenological reality that must be reckoned with when contemplating the meaning of meaning.

Almost all of the foregoing factors figured into the later phases of the overall project when Washoe herself took on the role of teacher and began to instruct the other chimpanzees in sign language, first in Oklahoma and later in Ellensburg, Washington. The most significant aspect of this development pertains to her teaching of Loulis, who, it will be recalled, had never been exposed to, let alone taught sign language by humans. Right from the start, Washoe began modeling, molding, and signing on her own body in exactly the way that the Gardners had used with her and that human parents use to teach deaf infants. The following excerpts from the Foutses' report are especially poignant:

During the first three days that they were together, Washoe often turned toward Loulis, signed COME, approached, and then grasped his arm and retrieved him. During the next five days, she signed COME, and only approached Loulis. Then after the first eight days, Washoe no longer approached but only signed COME while orientating and looking at Loulis until he responded by coming to her. COME was among the first signs that Loulis came to use. . . . Sometimes the first observation of a new sign involved direct imitation. For example, Loulis first used DRINK during a meal after Washoe used this sign in answer to a human care giver who had asked WHAT about a drink. As Washoe was signing DRINK, Loulis watched her and signed DRINK, himself. Washoe also modelled directly for Loulis. For example, she signed BRUSH and then brushed Loulis with a hairbrush. On another occasion, Washoe placed a small plastic chair in front of Loulis, and then signed CHAIR/SIT to him several times in succession, watching him closely throughout. (pp. 286–90)

It is interesting to note that Washoe herself actually learned new signs from the chimpanzees she was teaching. Initially she had been taught the verb/noun sign "cover" to designate a blanket. After Washoe moved to Oklahoma, however, the Gardners taught Moja, Tatu, and Dar the official ASL sign "blanket," which is quite unrelated in configuration to the sign "cover." When she was joined in Oklahoma by these younger chimpanzees, Washoe added this more precise sign to her vocabulary. In like manner, she acquired the sign "apple" from Moja, using it only to designate apples, as distinguished from the sign "fruit," which she used to indicate other fruit (p. 291).

Reflections on the Study

In offering some philosophical reflections on these concrete instances, patterns, and developments vis-à-vis the meaning of meaning, I shall again take my cue from the later Wittgenstein: in matters of linguistic meaning, one should begin with and stick to the facts of usage. That is, "Don't think, *look!*" I am not particularly interested in questions pertaining to whether chimpanzees can be said to "think" or to have a "conscious life." My concern is with the character and meaning of linguistic activity as embodied in the sign language behavior of the chimpanzees participating in this long-term experiment. The following discussion focuses on four major themes and concludes with some questions that need further exploration.

The first theme is that of the importance of the task-oriented character of language. This theme is highlighted by the dramatic difference between the experiments conducted according to the operant conditioning training program at Columbia University and that developed by the Gardners and Foutses in their respective family compounds. Learning language within the give-and-take and push-and-pull of daily life in a human household was absolutely crucial to the success of this entire project. The reason for the difference in results would appear to be that the natural, social environment provides a pragmatic and task-oriented context that serves as a vital component of the matrix out of which linguistic meaning emerges. In a deep sense, language is a tool, a device for getting things done in the physical and social dimensions of the world.

This pragmatic thrust of linguistic activity is clearly demonstrated in the incident wherein Loulis acquired the signs "come" and "gimme." The gradual shift from incorporating the signs into his babble or play to actually looking at the food, drink, or person involved in the linguistic context and orienting his use of the sign toward it exemplifies the transactional matrix out of which linguistic meaning evolves. Because human speakers, especially those studying language, generally focus exclusively on the conceptual or informational dimension of linguistic activity, they often fail to see the integral connection between it and the behavioral or practical dimension.

The employment of signs, whether oral or digital, becomes an inextricable strand in the fabric woven by shared goals and efforts. A more sophisticated example of this pragmatic thrust can be seen in an incident in which Washoe and Dar used the sign "tickle" as a means of redirecting Loulis's energetic activity away from harassment and toward a more socially acceptable mode of behavior. This practical function is humorously dramatized in Washoe's signing to herself in conjunction with her own clandestine and emergency activities as indicated earlier.

The second theme arising from the results of the study pertains to the gestural basis of linguistic meaning. Because oral expression is generally regarded as an abstract symbol that enables us to designate distant or absent aspects of reality, its connection to physical gesture and facial expression is frequently overlooked. It is more than likely that the development of written language greatly contributed to this tendency toward viewing language as a disembodied phenomenon. Nevertheless, it is of paramount importance to acknowledge the role of gesture not only in modulating linguistic meaning but in its very genesis. This role is extremely obvious in the dynamics of sign language, even with chimpanzees.

As was indicated early in the discussion of the study results, a kind of "somatic onomatopoeia" takes place in the acquisition of sign language, wherein signs tend to grow out of natural activities such as touching, eating, and smelling. In addition, this connection is clearly linked to the natural bodily interaction, or "cuddling," that takes place between adults and youngsters and leads to the somatic parallel to baby talk, namely, baby sign. Even when training Loulis to perform certain practical tasks, such as brushing his hair or sitting on a potty chair, Washoe incorporated the appropriate physical signs as she manipulated his body with her own.

Another aspect of this gestural dimension of the matrix out of which linguistic meaning emerges has to do with the actual molding of the learner's hands into the proper formation of the various signs being taught. Although this molding aspect is seemingly absent in the acquisition of oral language, it does factor in at the perceptual level in terms of the audial, visual, and oral cooperation necessary in order to reproduce the desired sounds. As previously noted, the making of audible language has become so familiar to adult speakers that they generally fail to notice the straightforwardly physiological anchorage of language. Speaking is, after all, a physical activity, whether it is done with the hands or with the mouth.

The phenomenon of pointing figures into our discussion because perhaps more than any other feature of linguistic activity and meaning, it focuses the fundamental gestural character of language. Linguistic philosophers used to be fond of maintaining that the basis of all language is ostensive definition. However, in light of Wittgenstein's insights, it has become evident that since the significance of pointing itself cannot be taught by means of pointing, the meaning of this gesture must be embedded in the connection between bodily activity and semantic reference. This connection is most clearly exhibited in the signs for indexical and demonstrative pronouns, "me," "you," "this," "that," "there," and "here." Initially all such terms must arise out of actual physical contact with the person, place, or thing in question.

The third theme that merits discussion is that of reciprocity. At the center of the push-and-pull and give-and-take, both tangible and intangible, comprising the matrix of linguistic meaning lies the game-like or playful dynamic of communicative activity. Built into the imitative drive or instinct of all primates is the capacity for reciprocal exchange and the anticipation of significance. Without this capacity, linguistic communication would be impossible, since it forms the arena within which games, songs, and the like arise and out of which develops actual training and conversation.

The importance of this dialogical factor can be seen in the crucial role played by the experimenters learning to mimic the natural movements and sounds of the chimpanzees. By incorporating such mimicry into their behavior, the experimenters were able to establish a common basis for empathetic understanding and mutual interchange between themselves and the chimpanzees. As researchers in these matters have only recently come to realize, the imitation that stands at the axis of linguistic acquisition is a two-way street; adults imitate infants and children as much as the young imitate adults. Such reciprocity helps create the commonality necessary to all learning.

Anyone who has paid attention to the early behavioral patterns of infants will have noticed their intense desire to be part of whatever is going on, especially linguistically. They quickly learn to follow and even anticipate speech patterns and melodies, exhibiting great delight in such exchanges. One-year-olds are notorious for interrupting adult mealtime conversations with a verbal barrage, followed by loud laughter and looking around for acceptance into the reciprocal activity. They even learn to use all the intonations of questions, declarations, jokes, and such, as when "talking" on a play telephone, for instance, well before they acquire much, if any, vocabulary. Such playful give-and-take is the ground out of which linguistic activity emerges and blossoms.

Eventually this imitative reciprocity develops into the ability to initiate creative verbal behavior of one's own, as is seen in the signings introduced by Washoe. Not only did such signs as "peekaboo" and "bib" arise from within task-oriented and gesture-based contexts, but they arose amid the dialogue surrounding shared activities. The reciprocal quality of language acquisition and practice is also seen in the fact that Washoe actually learned some signs from the youngsters whom she herself was teaching. Learning one's first language is never a matter of mere training, whether you are a human or a chimpanzee.

The fourth theme, which is perhaps a bit more controversial, concerns what might be designated the metaphorical aspect of language acquisition. It seems clear that at the outset all language is fundamentally vague and ambiguous, and any individual sign occurs within a context that is brim full of objects, qualities, and intentions. For instance, "Up?" said to an infant being lifted from its crib by its father every morning is associated with fresh sunlight, a smiling familiar face, a hug and a song, a change of diapers, and the morning feeding, as well as with the sensation of vertical movement. Thus this sign initially "means" all of these things. Only later and slowly do the extraneous things get sorted out by being given signs of their own in connection with different contextual associations and uses. At the outset all signs are metaphoric in a radical sense, in that they are part and parcel of the learner's reality rather than independent designator of it.

More specifically, a metaphor can be thought of as a linguistic device whereby a speaker juxtaposes or overlaps aspects of experienced reality that have not hitherto been related. Or a metaphoric expression can be viewed as a bending or stretching of the boundaries of a sign so as to include features of the world that it had not previously included. Washoe's modifications of the standard ASL signs clearly function as metaphors within her linguistic community. Also, all of the chimpanzees learned to modulate to some degree the signs they acquired, which clearly involves altering the conceptual categories directly associated with them.

Although this type of "poetic" metaphor can arise only after the acquisition of a more literal or specific vocabulary, the latter in turn can arise only out of the imprecision of initial use and reference. At the outset all linguistic signs are part of the reality in which they occur, and thus it is wiser and more helpful to think of them as continuing to function as such within that reality rather than as semantic pointers that have been abstracted out of it. In this way it is not necessary to wonder about the possibility and/or necessity of mental processes instigating or paralleling linguistic activity as a basis for its meaningfulness. The meaning of language, whether for chimpanzees or humans, would seem to lie within its use in context rather than behind or above it.

Finally, I will discuss a few questions about questions. It is as significant as it is puzzling that with all the work done concerning the chimpanzee's understanding and use of "wh-" questions, there is in this entire study only passing reference to the absence of "when" questions and no reference whatsoever to the question "why." Toward the end of their discussion of "wh-" questions, the Gardners indicated that while cross-fostered chimpanzees exhibit a developmental pattern comparable to that of human children for "who," "what," and "where," questions of "when" and "why" arise much later for the latter and "have not yet been studied for chimpanzees" (p. 236). More surprisingly, they also state that even those researchers working with human children have not yet presented data for the mastery of "how," "when," and "why" (p. 234).

It is interesting to speculate about such matters. It seems likely that temporal references, being less tangible, are more difficult to grasp and signify than spatial ones. I recall my own puzzlement and irritation at age four when my father answered my repeated question, "When will the movie start?" with the statement "In a minute." Jean Piaget and others have done numerous studies of how small children acquire spatial reasoning, but very little seems to have been done with temporal reasoning. One would like to think that the Foutses, who continue to direct the project of teaching sign language to chimpanzees, will pursue this issue in their future experiments.

The logic of "why" is, of course, even more difficult and significant. It is understandable that a question that asks for a reason for something would be a late arrival on the linguistic scene, but it is still disappointing and frustrating to note its complete absence from the chimpanzee vocabulary. I hope that this, too, will factor into the future experiments of those supervising this ongoing project, for here would seem to lie at least the down payment on the answers sought by those who search for the line of demarcation, or the absence thereof, between humans and chimpanzees. To be able to give a reason for something, such as one's own actions, would seem to constitute a sine qua non for being a moral as well as a rational being.

It strikes me as more than passing strange that the question "why," which is forever on the lips of nearly all young children, should in fact be a late linguistic acquisition. Moreover, since presumably the use and significance of this question must be learned from the adult practitioners of the language, it would seem that they themselves need to ask the question frequently of young children. However, it also seems intuitively odd to imagine oneself regularly interrogating a small child with a barrage of "why" questions, especially when generally one would be met either with no answer at all or with an equally perplexing "Because!" It seems that one has to know how to answer "why" questions before one can ask them, but how can you answer them if you do not already know how to ask them?

Actually, this dilemma, or vicious circle, constitutes but an instance of the comprehensive mystery known as language. In every case the situation seems to demand that one already have acquired language in order to acquire it. Once we are on square one, it is not very difficult to see how we get to square two and so forth. The difficulty—and it's a logical difficulty—lies in understanding how we get on the board in the first place, how we get from square zero to square one. In a deep sense, language acquisition remains a great mystery; it seems fundamentally impossible. At age one it seems clear that children will never acquire language, while at age two they are well on their way, and by six they are experts in their natural language without ever having had a formal lesson in it.

The answers to this mystery are to be found in the facts and principles presented by those doing research with chimpanzees and in the themes arising from them. Quite simply, to return to Wittgenstein's statements, chimpanzees do speak and we do understand them because, at least to a significant extent, we share a common "form of life," grounded as it is in gestural, reciprocal, and task-oriented embodiment. Perhaps the most definitive characteristic of human language is the fact that it is learned rather than instinctual. The simple but important truth of the effort to teach sign language to chimpanzees is not only that they have learned it but they have taught it to each other, if only to a limited extent.

2

Wolf Children and Language Acquisition

The majority of discussions of so-called feral children take place against the backdrop of questions concerning human nature vis-à-vis animal nature. More specifically, such discussions generally focus on the issue of how much and which aspects of human nature are innate and which are learned. Often this issue is cast in terms of what is called psychological heredity and whether or not it is a meaningful concept. At the outset it would seem safe to say that what we know as individual consciousness arises out of the matrix or loom of human experience by means of the interactions between the warp of genetic inheritance and the weft of social forces. In addition, it seems clear that humans are different from other animals in their capacity for such social interaction.

Since there is fairly general agreement that the axis of this uniquely human capacity is the power of speech, that both culture and individuality arise and are maintained by means of language, it is appropriate to pay special attention to this pivotal feature of human experience. My own interest in the speech potential of feral children is not as a means of achieving a final definition of human nature, however. It is, rather, to gain a better understanding of language in general and of how it serves to integrate physical behavior and cognitive activity in particular. My aim, in short, is to locate and explore the linguistic threshold that joins individual consciousness to shared social interaction.

A Survey of Cases

The best documentation of the legendary and historical accounts of the "wolf children" phenomenon is R. M. Zingg's essay "Feral Men and Extreme Cases of Isolation." In this article Zingg summarizes the history of thirty-one cases, ranging from rather doubtful ones to several that are clearly authentic. Beginning in 1344 with the wolf boy of Hesse, there are a dozen or so cases of children found running wild in various forests in western Europe, presumably keeping company with diverse animals such as wolves, bears, cows, and dogs. Some of these children made considerable progress in adjusting to human community, even to the point of acquiring human speech, while others hardly ever advanced beyond the status of domesticated animals. Since almost nothing is known about the circumstances of their infancy and separation from their families, it is difficult if not impossible to obtain much understanding from a study of these cases. The general consensus seems to be that those who subsequently acquired speech probably had been introduced to it prior to their separation.

At the beginning of the nineteenth century, a number of cases turned up about which there is much more documentation and exploration. Victor, the famous "wild boy" of Aveyron, was first written up in thoroughgoing fashion in 1801 by Jean-Marc-Gaspard Itard. Another boy, Kasper Hauser, became known in 1828 through the work of Anselm von Feuerbach. The "European" period in the history of such children came to a close around 1830, perhaps because the increasing population of western Europe made the chances for such eventualities ever less likely. At any rate, the most well-known and documented cases began to appear in India around the middle of the nineteenth century during the British colonial rule.

The initial but somewhat legendary accounts were reported by Major-General W. H. Sleeman in his *A Journey Through The Kingdom of Oude* in 1858. Most were cases of children having been carried off by wolves and "rediscovered" (or recaptured) some years later. Some of these children either managed to escape or died while in confinement. At least one learned to communicate through a simple sign language. E. B. Taylor made a comparative study of these children and two European cases in his essay "Wild Men and Beast Children." Nearly all of the children refused clothing and conventional human food and preferred to remain on all fours. None learned to talk in any way whatsoever. Several other wolf children were found in India between 1892 and 1898, one of whom was referred to as the "Baboon-Boy," but these cases were largely discredited by R. M. Zingg in 1940.

In 1920 two wolf girls, Amala and Kamala, were adopted and made the subject of a 150-page journal by J.A.L. Singh. The girls were also written about by W. N. Kellogg in the *American Journal of Psychology* between 1927 and 1934. Around 1930 there were two cases of leopard children in India and accounts of gazelle and monkey children in Africa as well. Along with these cases, two instances of prolonged isolation were discovered, Anna of Pennsylvania and Edith Riley of Ohio, reported by K. Davis and F. N. Maxwell, respectively, in the *American Journal of Psychology* in 1940. Although the latter differ widely in many respects from feral children, they do share in the crucial lack of human social and linguistic interaction and are thus highly relevant to the present study.

Anna of Pennsylvania, an illegitimate daughter born in 1932, was shut away on the second story of an isolated farmhouse for five years after having spent her first year in a kind of nursing home. Kept in a darkened room, receiving almost no human attention and very little food, Anna spent nearly all her time lying on a dirty mattress. When discovered in 1938, she was unable to stand on two feet and incapable of making the slightest sound. She could not focus her attention on any object or person for more than a few seconds, nor did she laugh or cry. After two years of normal attention and interaction, Anna showed great progress in being enculturated into human community, laughing, walking, feeding herself, and following simple verbal instructions.

Edith Riley was kept in a woodshed for a number of years, and at twelve years of age she was classified as a complete imbecile. Two years later, after being incorporated into a human family, she reached a normal level of intelligence. Such adjustment and progress became the primary evidence in the case against the hypothesis that feral children were initially abandoned because they possessed some serious intellectual deficiencies. Nearly all of those working closely with the children comprising these cases attest to the conclusion that the mental deficiencies of the feral children are the consequences, not the cause, of their isolation from human community. Lucian Malson's excellent book *Wolf Children and the Problem of Human Nature* provides a detailed account of the debate between these two points of view. Malson agrees with Arnold Gesell (*Wolf Child and Human Child*) and others that the intellectual elaboration of our experience of the world is indissolubly linked to the elaboration of our interpersonal relations. Also, the work of Bruno Bettelheim on the comparison of "Feral Children and Autistic Children" supports this general conclusion.

Two additional cases, while not strictly "wolf children," add extra depth to the foregoing survey. Early in 1977 the American public was made aware, through the popular media, of seven-year-old twin girls living in San Diego who apparently spoke a language they themselves had "invented." Virginia and Grace Kennedy were initially classified as retarded when they reached school age because they could not or would not speak to anyone except in what seemed to be pure gibberish. When psychologists began to suspect that the girls were actually communicating with each other in systematic fashion, even though no one else, including their parents, could understand them, they were brought to the speech therapy clinic at the San Diego Children's and Health Center.

It turned out that the language that the twins had created was a combination of English, German (their German-speaking grandmother lived with them), Spanish (their neighborhood included a number of Hispanic children), and their own "code words" strung together with a baby-talk pronunciation. Susan Taylor, chair of the Speech Pathology department at the hospital, said that this had proved "to be one of the few documented cases of idioglossia . . . a private communication that sometimes occurs between twins, but it's very rarely this developed or carried on to this age" (*US*, February 21, 1978, p. 42).

After being diagnosed, the girls were placed in separate special language classes and began to progress rapidly in the acquisition of English as their natural language. From these reports it is impossible to determine to what extent the twins were in any way isolated from adults and other children when they were very small. At any rate, their case provides an interesting comparison to those of the more specifically feral children already discussed.

Still another, somewhat different yet related case of attempted language acquisition after prolonged human isolationism is that of "Joe," first reported by Professor Lowell Bouma of the University of Georgia (National Language Conference, Washington, D.C., 1974). Having been born deaf, Joe received a powerful hearing aid and was introduced to language for the first time at the age of thirty-nine. At the outset it seemed extremely unlikely that he would be able to learn to speak, since he was far behind what was usually regarded as the "critical age" for language acquisition. Some success had been reported with much younger people who were enabled to hear after puberty, as in the celebrated case of Genie (Curtiss et al., *Language* 50, pp. 528–54).

Before being fitted with his hearing aid, Joe had learned to say the words "mama," "papa," and "bye," as well as the names of his siblings. In his initial exposure to language at a small training center, Joe was able to acquire about fifty words with varying degrees of accuracy. Most of these words were nouns referring to objects in his environment, such as clothing, parts of the body, and various animals. He also used the verbs "go," "stop," "drive," and "iron," along with the adjectives "hot" and "fat" and the pronouns "you" and "me." Joe spoke with the staff and children at the training center, and they with him, in much the same way children and adults normally converse with one another. His pronunciation ability was limited by some degree of sound-producing muscular retardation.

Since Joe had been communicating for almost forty years by means of a privately developed gross-gesture system, he now rarely used language without these gestures and only infrequently used oral language spontaneously, even though he was highly motivated to acquire speech.

Like normal children learning language, Joe seemed to enjoy naming various items in his environment, although he usually needed to be prompted to do so. In addition, most of his utterances were one-word sentences; for example, the word "fish" would variously mean "That's a fish," "That man is fishing," or "There's a place for fishing." In at least one instance Joe used the word "pig" metaphorically to refer jokingly to a friend who had not put his napkin on his plate after finishing a meal. This ability to extend or twist the original meaning of a word to perform a different function is as common among early learners of language as it is necessary to the nature of language itself.

Joe also frequently overgeneralized by using a word to refer to items that, while similar in some respect to those designated by the term, are actually referred to by other terms. "Doggie" was used to designate other four-legged creatures, and "watch" to name all sorts of timepieces. Again, not only is this a common and understandable "mistake," but it is also the basis for all analogical insight and reasoning, both in children and adults. Joe was also able to put together two-word sentences in adjectival construction, such as "baby dog" and "Joe's shoes." He was not able, however, to put together two-word sentences involving verbs and nouns. Yet with special training and promptings, he was able to learn specific sentences like "Joe drive car." Nevertheless, when he tried to say sentences like "Joe drive Ginger's car," he would frequently mix up the word order.

Those working with Joe were of the opinion that at best his level of speech would always be more similar to that of a person learning a second language than to normal natural language acquisition, since he had already learned how to communicate through gesture and function as an adult before learning to speak. Thus his "language" remains a kind of sophisticated "code." On the other hand, it seems at least paradoxical, if not downright contradictory, to say that one can learn a second language even though one has not as yet really acquired a first.

A Closer Look at Special Cases

The case of Kasper Hauser is especially interesting because he represents a child who stands midway between normal children and the extreme "wild" or wolf children discussed in the previous section. Evidently, as was revealed after his death, Kasper was the son of the niece of Napoleon's wife, Josephine, and had been raised in minimally human fashion by caretakers. He turned up one day in 1828 in Nuremberg, fully dressed and carrying a number of personal belongings, at the age of seventeen. He could write his name, speak a few simple sentences, and play with small objects. Kasper seemed to have the mind of a three-year-old child. He walked in a drifting manner, cried and laughed a great deal, loved to see horses, and could write simple numbers, letters, and his name on paper. Feuerbach described him as one who "could have been taken for a creature from another planet, having landed miraculously on earth" (*Kasper Hauser*, 1832).

After two months of living in a cell in the soldiers' garrison, Kasper went to live in the home of Dr. Daumer, a local citizen who took pity on him. There he grew stronger, more agile, and took to drawing instead of playing with small toys. In everything he was abnormally tidy. Kasper was extremely docile, seemed to have no interest in or awareness of sexuality, could see very well in the dark, disliked bright sunlight, had little sense of perspective, and was never able to comprehend how mirrors work. Moreover, he seemed unable to tell the difference between dreams and reality when telling stories, and had a keen sense of hearing except for clocks and church bells. Similarly, he greatly enjoyed music, especially loud drums, but when he watched military parades from his window, he seemed terrified by the noise.

Various efforts were made to educate Kasper in speaking, writing, and arithmetic. In the beginning he learned to use the infinitive form of verbs and used nouns as direct referents without any inflections provided by prefix, suffix, and prepositions. In addition, Kasper spoke in clauses that were rarely connected grammatically with one another and seems never to have mastered the use of the imperative and subjunctive modes. He did, however, make ample use of the interrogative mode, constantly asking simple and direct questions like "Who made the tree?," "Where is my soul?," and "Why doesn't God answer my prayers?"

There are two especially interesting features of Kasper's speech acquisition that warrant mention. One is his tendency to use one noun to refer to all the members of a class of which the noun's referent is a member. For example, he used the term "berg" (mountain) to describe anything that was tall. This is similar to a normal child's early tendency to call all men "Daddy," or all four-legged creatures "bow wow" or "moo cow." There is no indication in Feuerbach's account that Kasper indulged in the opposite tendency, as most small children do, of using a general term as a proper name for an individual entity within that general category. What is especially interesting about the former practice is that it is surely related to the use and development of metaphor in adult speech. The extension of a category or concept so as to include entities that are not normally included or referred to thereby is a fundamental skill with respect to all language and thought. There is, after all, a basic similarity between mountains and other tall things, and the ability to recognize and articulate this analogical connection is a key to human intelligence.

By way of example, consider the following speech-act of my youngest son when he was sixteen months old. He was sitting on my lap holding a basketball as we watched a game on television. During a break in the action, he looked up at me, smiled, held up the ball, and asked, "Apple?" He then took an imaginary bite out of the ball. We both enjoyed this joke, but I still marvel at any child's ability not only to recognize similarities and express them in analogies and metaphors, but to make a joke out of it at the same time. Unfortunately, it seems that Kasper never engaged in language as a form of humor.

A second important parallel between Kasper's acquisition of language and that of normal children pertains to the use of the term "I." Kasper, according to Feuerbach, generally referred to himself in the third person, either as "Kasper" or "me," and came to use the first person very slowly. Not only is this self-referential pattern typical of normal children as well, but it also reflects the relational character of self-awareness. As George Herbert Mead so clearly delineated, the self is a social reality, created out of the interaction between an incipient or growing person and his or her significant others. This emergence of self-awareness is reflected in the linguistic patterns displayed in our use of the third- and first-person pronouns. We, like Kasper, grow into our awareness of our own selves as acting subjects in relation to others by means of our interaction with them in our common world.

A friend of mine tells the story of his three-year-old son, who, upon moving to a new home, went next door to meet the new neighbor. The neighbor asked the youngster if he had any brothers. After thinking about it for a few moments, my friend's son replied, "No, but I have two sisters, and they have a brother, and that's me!" Such roundabout awareness of one's own place in the world, as mediated through relationship to others, is undoubtedly what Kasper experienced, and it was expressed in the difficulty he had in learning to use the first-person pronoun "I."

Next, let us return to the case of the young Indian girl Kamala. The story of the discovery of two "wolf girls" in 1920 by the Reverend Singh is quite amazing in and of itself. The young girls were actually living in a cave with several adult wolves and two cubs and displayed animal-like behavior, such as leaping around on all fours, panting, and baring their teeth. It was apparent that the girls were being protected by the adult wolves as if they were truly wolf cubs. After much confusion and several time lapses, Reverend Singh was able to bring the girls, whom he named Amala and Kamala, to his orphanage in Midnapore. Amala, the smaller of the two, was judged to be about one-and-a-half years old, while the larger Kamala appeared to be at least eight.

Both of the girls suffered from photophobia and day blindness, coming to life at night, howling and rapidly pacing up and down, either on their knees and elbows or on hands and feet. They lapped liquids and ate only meat. In addition, they snarled and arched their backs when approached by humans. Amala died after one year from nephritis and generalized edema. Kamala also died of the same condition roughly eight years later. A record of the latter's psycho-physical development was kept by Singh and reported by Arnold Gesell in his book *Wolf Child and Human Child.*

Kamala gradually learned to reach for her food, and after six years she was able to walk in an upright posture. Slowly she became more relaxed and acquired socially related behavior, such as washing and bathing, looking after small children and alerting nurses when they were crying, and performing small tasks around the farm. Her progress suffered a temporary setback when her sister Amala died. She cried for the first time and refused to eat or drink for two days. Soon, however, she grew fond of Mrs. Singh, who would massage her muscles in order to loosen her joints. Once she actually took Mrs. Singh's hands and showed her where she wished to be massaged. In addition, Kamala gradually grew to prefer the daylight to the night and wanted to sleep near other children at night. She even became quite modest, refusing to leave the dormitory without being dressed.

Within a year Kamala spoke two words, "ma" to designate Mrs. Singh and "bhoo" as an expression of hunger or thirst. After two years she could signal yes and no by nodding or shaking her head and could also say "hoo" when nodding yes. In 1924 she asked for rice with the sound "bha" and used "Am jab" to say "I want." In addition to eventually acquiring about fifty words, including the names of the main people with whom she had to do, she could also understand verbal instructions and made ample use of various sign-signals whenever she did not know a particular word. To a significant degree, Kamala can be said to have achieved membership in a human community and to have acquired language parallel to that of a normal two-year-old human child.

The case of Victor is by far the most extreme example of isolation from human society about which there is extensive information concerning development after being brought into human community. Victor, so named by his eventual guardian and teacher, Jean Itard, was first sighted in 1797 in the woods near Tarn, France. After several captures and escapes, he was finally brought to various hospitals, having been officially classified as a "congenital idiot." Itard, however, argued that his condition was the result of having been deprived of normal human interaction, and he set about to prove this hypothesis by taking Victor to his institute for study and training. It seems that next to nothing was or is known about Victor's origin or early survival. At the time of capture he was about ten years old, and when he was finally brought to Itard's institute in Paris he was about twelve.

Although Victor moved about on two legs and used his hands to get food to his mouth, he murmured while he ate, was subject to sudden fits of anger, was especially fond of fires, slept according to the sun, and tried constantly to escape. His moods swung from nervous excitement to complete passivity. At night he would stare long and admiringly at the moon. His only manual skill was shelling beans, and he showed no interest in participating in other children's activities or imitating any human behavior. Moreover, he showed no interest in or capacity for sexual arousal and displayed a remarkable insensitivity to pain and surrounding odors, sounds, and events. His powers of concentration were very poor, and he was surprisingly helpless when it came to seemingly simple and natural physical tasks, such as climbing up onto a chair to reach something he wanted. Victor made no distinguishable sounds, and his facial expression would alternate rapidly between a sullen scowl and a curious sneer that may have been an effort to smile.

In the early years of his training under Itard, Victor interacted with his caretakers, visitors, and others at the institute like a kind of domesticated animal. He learned to dress himself, hold out his plate for food, show people to the door, ride in a wheelbarrow, and be taken on regular walks. He became increasingly sensitive to heat and cold, different sorts of food, and also became very fond of those who looked after him.

Victor's intellectual development, however, seemed to lag far behind his physical and social adaptation. For several years he remained totally unresponsive to all phonetic sounds except the vowel "o," and it was for this reason that Itard give him the name Victor. Eventually Victor learned to pronounce all the vowels except "u" and three consonants, including "l," which was the first letter of his first real word, "lait" (milk). Although he did not use the word to ask for milk, he did use it as a sort of exclamation of pleasure when he was given milk to drink. Itard constructed an elaborate system of boards with pictures of objects on them so that Victor could cover each with the appropriate object as he learned to recognize them. He eventually progressed to using letters of the alphabet and then to whole words for the things on the boards. Thus Victor came to recognize words in written form and to speak some of them within the context of the board games, including the word "lait." Nevertheless, Itard was perpetually frustrated in his efforts to get Victor to use the word for milk when he actually wanted to have some milk.

After some six years at the institute, Victor had become increasingly socialized in terms of both behavior and habits, as well as in terms of emotions and personal relations. He became eager to learn and to please, much like a normal human child, although at first his learning seems to have closely resembled the conditioning of pigeons and mice by present-day behavioral psychologists. Gradually, though, Victor began to grasp conceptual distinctions, objects and the relations between them, and the notion of action (verbs). Although he never learned to speak, he did learn to write, expressing his feelings and wishes by spelling out words with letters. It seems clear that it no longer made sense to classify Victor as an idiot. When he turned eighteen, Itard turned Victor entirely over to the keeping of Madame Guerin, the woman who had served as his governess, and he lived with her in the annex of the institute until he died at the age of forty. It is interesting to note that the autopsy performed on Victor after his death revealed no evidence of any sort of brain damage.

Itard's Methodology

Jean Itard kept a detailed account of his efforts to enable Victor to acquire speech. The following is his initial summary of the description of Victor given by a Professor Pinel, based on his early examinations:

> The author of the report exhibited him to us as incapable of attention . . . and consequently of all the operations of the mind which depend on it; destitute of memory, judgement, even of a disposition to imitation; and so bounded were his ideas, even those that related to his immediate wants, that he could not open a door, nor get on a chair to obtain the food which was put out of the reach of his hand; in short, destitute of every means of communication, attaching neither expression nor intention to the gestures and motions of his body, passing with rapidity, and without any apparent motive, from a state of profound melancholy, to bursts of the most immoderate laughter; insensible to every feature of moral affection, his discernment was never excited but by the stimulus of gluttony; his pleasure, an agreeable sensation of the organs of taste, his intelligence, a susceptibility of producing incoherent ideas, connected with his physical wants; in a word, his whole existence was a life purely animal. (Malson, p. 98)

Itard set for himself and Victor five educational goals. The first was "to attach to him a social life by rendering it more pleasant . . . than that which he was then leading and, above all, more analogous to the mode of existence that he was about to quit" (p. 102). It is to Itard's credit that he realized that to alter Victor's form of life from top to bottom too abruptly would only confuse and harm him. Rather, Itard sought to "associate" Victor's old habits with his new existence in such a way as to render the latter more agreeable to him. At the same time, Itard instinctively understood that linguistic acquisition is inextricably bound up within the socialization process through imitation, conditioning, and interaction.

The second goal was to "awaken the nervous sensibility by . . . powerful stimulants and . . . lively affections of the mind" (p. 105). Itard was convinced that Victor's prolonged exposure to the natural elements, together with his overly active muscular outdoor life, had rendered him insensitive to the varying degrees of temperature, sound, and feeling. In the early days of his "captivity," Victor was able to endure extremes of heat and cold, loud noises, and various other deprivations without showing any real awareness of them. After three months Itard's efforts to evoke some perceptual and emotional sensitivity in Victor began to work. In a word, he became rather "refined," especially in his choice of foods and manner of eating. It is debatable just how necessary these changes were to Victor's "education," though it cannot be denied that to some degree such things surely do factor into what it means to become a human being.

Third, Itard sought to "extend the sphere of his ideas by giving him new wants, and multiplying his relations and connections with surround objects" (p. 111). Here again we see the wisdom of Itard's instincts, since by stimulating wants in relation to interaction with the multivarious elements of the environment, he was developing Victor's intentionality, his meaningful direction toward and within the world around him. This "existential vector" is perhaps the most salient characteristic of the human-way-of-being-in-the-world. Moreover, to engage the different aspects of one's environment in order to accomplish certain tasks in cooperation with other persons is truly the seed plot for language acquisition. After all, one speaks to and with others in order to accomplish specific tasks in one's life and in one's surroundings.

To accomplish this goal, Itard devised many experiments and practices aimed at multiplying Victor's pleasures by way of broadening his horizons. In each case "I had found out a *pleasure* for him; I had only repeat it a certain number of times in order to convert it into a *want*" (p. 113). In addition to frequent walks, both in town and in the country, Victor was encouraged to form relationships with a diversity of personages in and around the hospital. He became especially fond of Madame Guerin, his governess, as well as of Itard himself.

Itard's fourth goal for Victor was to "lead him to the use of speech by subjecting him to the necessity of imitation" (p. 116). Although Itard came to deem his efforts in this direction an abysmal failure, he nonetheless was very specific in his account of his methodology. Victor's ability to discern various sounds seemed to be erratic, and the physiological manipulations required for sound production and enunciation appeared to be beyond his capacities, perhaps because of his relatively advanced age. As noted earlier, he did respond consistently to the vowel "o," leading Itard to choose Victor for his name. He also came to understand the word "non" (no), most likely building on the sound analogy, and Itard made ample use of this word in his training sessions.

Itard took every opportunity to exclaim "eau" (water) whenever Victor was given water, but although he engaged in various forms of animation in these situations, Victor never uttered any sound that in any way resembled this word. Itard then shifted to the word "lait" (milk), and after four days of frequent repetition, Victor began to utter the word incessantly. However, after he had observed that Victor always only uttered the word "lait" upon receiving his milk, rather than as a means of asking for it, Itard came to the following somewhat surprising and premature conclusion:

> If this word had been uttered before the thing that he desired had been granted, my object would have been nearly accomplished: then the true use of speech would have been soon acquired by Victor; a point of communication would have been established between him and me, and the most rapid progress must necessarily have ensued. Instead of this I had obtained only an expression of the pleasure which he felt, insignificant as it related to himself, and useless to me. (p. 122)

This conclusion strikes me as surprising and premature because on the basis of my own rather careful observation of my own children, it seems that the exclamatory stage generally precedes the requesting stage in the use of nearly any term. Itard contrasts Victor's lack of speaking ability to his exceptional capacity for a kind of pantomime behavior, which he calls a "language of action." Nearly all of the daily tasks and activities comprising his life were carried out by means of specific requests being acted out by Victor and his significant others. His governess, for example, would hold up the water pitcher, show that it was empty, and hand it to Victor. He, in turn, would go to the pump and fill the pitcher with water. Itard remained of the opinion that eventually this sort of communication would become insufficient for Victor's needs and would drive him to the use of verbal signs. Unfortunately, he hypothesized that Victor, like all children, would develop in this direction as the result of "a multitude of reasonings and even abstractions" (p. 126). It seems more likely that children initially learn where and when to apply specific symbols through constant correction and increasing success in the push-and-pull of everyday life.

Next, as previously mentioned, Itard hung movable pictures of objects on a large board and found that Victor soon was able to replace the figures in their proper order after Itard had removed them. Then he hit on the idea of placing the written names of the objects in these pictures beneath them on the board as well; by this association he hoped to teach Victor the signs for the objects. However, even though deaf and mute children had been taught the meaning of the signs in this manner, "it was not the same with Victor, who, not withstanding the most frequent repetitions, not withstanding the protracted exhibition of the thing below the name belonging to it, could never know the thing by the word" (p. 130).

Later on, Itard constructed the same sort of board with nails on which to hang the letters of the alphabet. After observation and some practice, Victor learned to replace all the letters in their appropriate places after they had been removed. However, he contrived to do so by making sure that the letters remained in the order in which they had been taken off the board and handed to him. Next, Itard began to associate the letters of the word "lait" with Victor's morning milk, and very soon he himself was able to arrange the letters so as to spell "lait" whenever he was given milk. Finally, Victor actually came to be able to spell out the world "lait" with the letters before he received his milk. Thus he was able to "write" the word as a way of requesting the milk, even though he never came to be able to ask for it through oral language. After nine months Itard concluded "that the child known under the name of the Savage of Aveyron is endowed with the free exercise of all his senses; that he gives continual proofs of attention, reflection and memory; that he is able to compare, discern, and judge, and apply in short all the faculties of his understanding to the objects which are connected with his instruction" (p. 137).

Seven years later, in 1806, Itard wrote a second report on his continued educational experiments with Victor. One major focus during this period was the heightening of Victor's sense of hearing so as to make him more sensitive to the nuances of the human voice in speech. While blindfolded, he was taught to raise, respectively, different fingers upon hearing different sounds, especially those of the vowels. Although this worked rather well, the pleasure Victor received from the gamelike procedure soon led to outbursts of laughter, which in turn led to finger-slapping disciplinary measures on

Itard's part. These difficulties eventually undermined the whole experiment.

Itard next turned his attention to Victor's visual abilities and was able to teach him to "read" and "write" in the sense that he could recognize and reproduce the appropriate letters on request. However, he never came to comprehend the meaning of any of the words he "learned" in this way, as was evidenced by the fact that he did not connect any of them with the objects or events in his daily environment. Itard developed parallel experiments and lessons in relation to Victor's sense of touch, and even smell, with differing degrees of success.

They then returned to the label game, in which Victor was able to associate the names on cards with various objects in his room, but with which he had been unable to learn to use these labels to request an object, such as a glass of milk. Itard was disappointed to discover that Victor could not locate objects other than those with which he had formed his original associations, even when the two objects were nearly identical. Clearly, Victor related to the labels as proper names rather than as symbols designating a type or class of objects.

The next series of lessons was aimed at teaching Victor to recognize and identify classes of objects. Here, too, the usual difficulties were encountered, since he exhibited a strong tendency to "stretch" a class name to include a wide range of items only remotely resembling one another. It should be noted once again that this overextension phenomenon continues to be the basis for all metaphorical and analogical insight and expression in every language. After a while, however, Victor was able to tighten the range of his application of terms so as to conform roughly to that of ordinary usage. This was accomplished by developing a sequence of exercises aimed at helping Victor distinguish parts from wholes, smaller objects from each other, and abstractions such as "big" and "small." Victor displayed a great deal of fortitude and intelligence in learning to accomplish these tasks. He was even able to grasp the difference between verbs and nouns and developed an understanding of quite a number of different verbs.

Finally, Itard instructed Victor in writing, first by having him trace out words already written on the chalkboard and then by having him imitate Itard himself as he drew lines on the chalkboard. This imitation process worked fairly well, and Itard concluded, "By the end of a few months Victor could copy words whose meanings he already knew and very soon afterwards he could produce them from memory and finally make use of his writing, shapeless as it was, to express his needs, to ask for the wherewithal to satisfy them and by the same means to understand the needs and wishes of others" (p. 165).

Building on this and other writing experience, Itard made one last effort to bring Victor to speech. Having taken great pains to sensitize and exercise Victor's facial muscles, including his lips, tongue, and vocal cords, Itard sought intently for Victor to connect up various sounds with the words he could read and write — but to no avail. Itard concluded his second and final report with some general comments on Victor's emotional and intellectual growth. While acknowledging his own frustration over not being able to bring Victor speech, he expressed great satisfaction with the boy's development in personal relationships and cognitive skills. He attributed Victor's lack of speech to his having been deprived of social and linguistic interaction before he reached puberty. The speech functions of the brain seemed simply to have atrophied as a result of this prolonged isolation. Itard credited Victor's relational and cognitive development to his native capacities as stimulated by personal interaction and Itard's own educational program. In my own view, while the latter was creative and advanced, Itard's social and psychological perspectives were backward and reprehensible. Often his reward and punishment techniques were downright medieval and immoral, but such topics are beyond the scope of this study.

In drawing conclusions, it must be acknowledged that it is not possible to demonstrate any hard and fast knowledge with respect to the cognitive and linguistic capacities of so-called wolf children. Little if anything was, or indeed could be, done to provide the sorts of experimental controls necessary for any replicable results or solid inferences. Moreover, the actual data available in most cases are sketchy at best. With a few exceptions, the records kept were both thin and conflicting, leaving us room for a great deal of speculation and possible misunderstanding. The only real exception here is Itard's record of his experiments and lessons with Victor. However, even these records are polemical in character and far from systematic in nature. It is possible, nonetheless, to gain some degree of understanding from a careful examination of Itard's work.

In general it is safe to say that the information we have on feral children corroborates contemporary theory and experimentation concerning the importance of linguistic experiences matching physiological maturation processes and levels. It is amply clear that children who suffer extreme isolation and thus are not extensively exposed to language within the first twelve years or so seem to be beyond the language "threshold" or temporal "window." In spite of the fact that many of these children were able to learn other aspects of human behavior, for the most part they never got beyond the level of domesticated animals linguistically. Although some of this difficulty may be the result of deep psychic trauma, there is good reason to believe that there exists a relatively firm language threshold beyond which the acquisition of speech at the level of a "mother tongue" becomes essentially impossible.

The case of Victor is an exception to this general rule, since although he was unable to acquire oral speech he is reported as having learned how to communicate through written words. It is possible that his vocal equipment was damaged or itself had passed beyond some maturation boundary before he was exposed to speech. In this regard Victor is somewhat similar to the chimpanzees that have been taught the sign language of the deaf and seem to be able to communicate in this way. Apparently chimpanzees do not have the physical mechanism or brain capacity with which to produce and shape the range of sounds necessary to oral language. Like Victor, however, they seem to have sufficient cognitive ability for at least minimal symbolic communication. Another dimension of this whole issue involves the importance of bodily communication, since symbolic activities of all kinds seem to emerge out of body language and gesture.

As Maurice Merleau-Ponty has indicated in his highly insightful and influential work *Phenomenology of Perception,* somatic rationality and communication provide the axis around which all forms of symbolic activity revolve. Conventional gestures, signals, speech, and even written language all arise out of the embodied character of our human existence. To the degree to which each of the children presented in this chapter can be said to have come to participate in human social intercourse, to that degree it is also evident that this participation came about as the result of their having been placed within a context where such interaction was physically modeled and encouraged. Moreover, as with both Joe and Victor, this somatic dimension grew to be the primary means of communication, since speech seems to have systematically evaded them. There is no fixed line of demarcation, after all, between symbols and signs on the one hand and gestures and "body" language on the other. This much, at least, the semioticists have taught us.

Perhaps the most obvious and significant factor in the cases of isolation and deprivation is the absence of direct human social interaction. In this sense language is, after all, a social reality. The social context constitutes both the foundation and the framework for all linguistic activity and acquisition, since it provides their necessary conditions and their formative influences. One of the unique features of language is that it is already here when each of us arrives on the scene; it is a general fact of human reality in the same way our physical embodiment is. However, language also evolves and thereby shapes our individual speech acquisitions and patterns in an ongoing manner. In the cases discussed in this chapter, there is a marked difference in the achievements, both in communication and otherwise, between those children who were brought within some sort of family environment and those who were not. Much of this difference hinges, to be sure, on the psychological and emotional value of stimulation, a sense of belonging, and a sense of being valued. This is especially clear in the cases of Emily, Anna, and Victor.

In addition to such factors, however, there is the cruciality of the task-oriented character of family life. In the push-and-pull of everyday life at the family level, there is a continuous flow of things that have to be done: get this, go there, do that, and so on. It is the warp and weft provided by such activity that weaves the fabric within which language emerges. As Wittgenstein so clearly saw and stressed, people speak in order to—and as they—accomplish specific tasks in their shared world, and thus speech can only be acquired within the give-and-take of such social interaction. In the cases of Kamala, Kasper, and Victor, there is a strong correlation between the extent to which they were brought within the social interactivity of the adults surrounding them, together with the corresponding "language games," and the degree to which they came to acquire speech. Such incorporation into the social fabric of the speaking community triggers both individual intentionality and linguistic activity. The writings of George Herbert Mead, especially in *On Social Psychology*, show how this is the case from a theoretic standpoint. The experiences of the wolf children illustrate and demonstrate it from an experiential standpoint.

In all of these cases, nevertheless, it must not go unacknowledged that the business of acquiring language is not an all-or-nothing proposition; it is, rather, a matter of degree. Not only do all children go through various stages of proficiency in which they develop and overcome certain problematic patterns, but the feral children under discussion here also exhibited specific developmental stages, thresholds, and ultimate limits in their struggles to communicate and understand symbolically. Kamala and Kasper may be thought of as representing something like the opposite extremes in this regard, while Victor stands somewhere in the middle. There are similarities between acquiring one's own natural language and obtaining fluency in another language. When can a person be said to be fluent in a foreign language? Clearly there are degrees of fluency in such cases. In like manner, the feral children seem to sort out at various points along the scale of fluency in original acquisition. Perhaps it is fair to say that they get "stuck" at one point or another. At any rate, in their cases, unlike the situation with normal children over six years of age, it remains meaningful to speak of degrees of fluency with respect to their first language.

Finally, it can be remarked that as a general pattern in these cases, the child came to self-awareness late, if at all, as a result of relational and linguistic interaction. Imitative activity would seem to give rise to participatory activity, which in turn yields individual intentionality. Only later, however, does one learn to turn this vectorial intentionality back on one's self so as to produce self-consciousness. Normal children generally progress from referring to themselves by what others call them, that is, their first name, through objective case references, "me," to first-person assertions using "I." This general progression appears to have been operative in some of the cases of feral children. The overall pattern once again underlines the social character and direction of linguistic activity in general and of language acquisition in particular.

The foregoing explorations constitute nothing but an initial foray into rare and largely unknown regions in an effort to chart the broad contours of the language threshold. When bolstered by an examination of even more cases, which we hope will be more carefully documented, explorations of the type offered here may cast further light on the nature of this elusive but ever so crucial threshold.

3

The Case of Helen Keller

The overarching conclusion toward which this book points is that both linguistic meaning and human cognition are, contrary to both traditional and modern epistemologists, grounded in and achieved by means of the body. In short, to mean and to know are inseparable from embodied human activity. This chapter uses the familiar story of Helen Keller to explore three themes—language, truth, and body— in relation to a single phenomenon, namely, language acquisition. For in this extremely commonplace yet fundamentally mysterious process, it is particularly easy to see how inextricably incorporated language and knowledge are into our somatic experience.

Skinner, Chomsky, and Helen Keller

The discussion over how a child's acquisition of its natural language is accomplished has centered in the debate between contemporary empiricists, such as B. F. Skinner, and rationalists, such as Noam Chomsky. Skinner seeks to explain "verbal behavior," in his book by that name, strictly on the basis of operant conditioning processes. The child imitates those who speak and is rewarded for so doing and thus learns to speak. For Skinner, all learning is simply a complex form of physical behavior. Chomsky and others have demonstrated rather conclusively that Skinner's explanation is unable to account for two obvious facts, namely, that (1) children are as much imitated by the speakers around them as they themselves imitate others, and (2) children both make and understand linguistic utterances that they have never encountered previously.

Chomsky has argued that we are born with a universal grammar, one that operates according to certain transformational rules already implanted in the circuitry of our brains. Thus, all natural languages are the product of a common "deep structure" that represents the "language of thought" itself. This form of contemporary rationalism, sometimes referred to as "structuralism," harkens back to Plato's notion of recollection and Descartes's concept of innate ideas. Chomsky's as-yet-unformulated rules by means of which all languages are generated are perhaps more similar to Kant's "categories of understanding."

The difficulty with all this, however, is that in addition to the fact that these universal rules remain elusive to the best efforts of Chomsky and his cohorts, the entire schema is presented as if human speakers were not embodied. Human physicality and activity are simply given no place in the entire process of language acquisition. While Skinner allows speech to be overdetermined by somatic factors, albeit in relatively passive fashion, Chomsky requires it to be overdetermined by intellectual principles. His explanation falls victim to all the pitfalls of modern intellectualist epistemology.

An especially poignant and instructive case in point is that of Helen Keller. Her achievement is particularly significant because she came to experience meaning and to know the world around her by means of tactile sign language. Although her situation as a deaf-mute was uniquely dramatic and atypical, it was essentially no different from that of all children who become members of a speaking community through verbal interaction with those around them.

Skinnerian behaviorism fails to explain how Helen Keller acquired language because it has no way to account for her ability to move beyond the apelike stage of imitation with respect to the sign language to which her teacher, Annie Sullivan, had introduced her. Keller learned many signs and could "repeat" them in relation to their appropriate objects fairly consistently. At first, however, she did not seem to "understand" anything that Sullivan signed to her, nor did she ever initiate any signing in order to "say" anything herself. Such a situation could have gone on forever and, according to strict operant conditioning theory, could only have done so. Nevertheless, one day by the pumphouse something more than mere imitation and conditioning transpired.

On the other side of the ledger, Chomsky's structuralism fails to explain Helen Keller's achievement because it separates it from her embodied behavior. To say that acquiring one's natural language is more than mere behavior does not entail that it is less. In fact, to extricate Keller's breakthrough from its physical and social setting by focusing on an intellectual pattern, as Chomsky's theory necessitates, is to render it inexplicable in principle as well as humanly unrealistic. The acquisition of language is neither exclusively a function of the body nor one of the mind; rather, it is the result of the interaction between the two in a concrete and evolving context.

Helen Keller herself claimed that it was by becoming a member of the speaking community that she entered the human race (see her account in her book *Teacher*). Prior to this event, she was, in her own words, a mere "phantom" who responded to tactile stimuli without ever engaging in an "intentional" act as a human being. Though atypical in its specific form, her acquisition of language dramatizes the role of embodiment as well as that of speech in establishing the meaning of being human. For Helen Keller's language was distinctively, though not uniquely, a somatic affair, and thus, so was her cognitivity.

It is interesting and enlightening to think of sign language as a kind of onomatopoeia in which the sign and that signified are essentially united. Owen Barfield and others have argued that all language flows from such primordial unity of speaker, sound, and object (see Barfield's *Poetic Diction*, especially chapter 4). In Helen Keller's case this unity was intensely focused because of the proximity, indeed identity, among these three dimensions of human existence. Nevertheless, each and every child who learns to speak passes through essentially the same experience, though less dramatically.

Cassirer, Percy, and Helen Keller

Philosophers of language have frequently been fascinated by the event and the accounts thereof wherein Helen Keller achieved her linguistic breakthrough and entered the speaking community. Ernst Cassirer, in seeking to extend his neo-Kantian understanding of the relationship between language and thought, described what happened on the Keller farm in Tuscumbia, Alabama, in 1887 in terms of a new "level of consciousness." He concluded that Helen Keller realized that the symbol w-a-t-e-r, spelled into her hand by teacher Annie Sullivan, served a "representational function." "When the representative function of names has thus dawned on a child, his whole inner attitude toward reality has changed—a fundamentally new relation between subject and object has come into being. Only now do the objects which hitherto acted directly on the emotions begin in a sense to recede into the distance . . . where they can be 'looked at' (*Philosophy of Symbolic Forms,* vol. 3, p. 113).

It is significant that Cassirer quotes from Sullivan's more or less "objective" account rather than from Helen Keller's own, more "subjective" statement of what transpired. Here is the crucial paragraph in Annie Sullivan's words:

> We went out to the pump-house, and I made Helen hold her mug under the spout while I pumped. As the cold water gushed forth, filling the mug, I spelled "w-a-t-e-r" in Helen's free hand. The word coming so close upon the sensation of cold water rushing over her hand seemed to startle her. She dropped the mug and stood as one transfixed. A new light came into her face. She spelled "water" several times. Then she dropped on the ground and asked for its name and pointed to the pump and the trellis, and suddenly turning round she asked for my name. I spelled "Teacher." Just then the nurse brought Helen's little sister into the pump-house, and Helen spelled "baby" and pointed to the nurse. All the way back to the house she was highly excited, and learned the name of every object she touched, so that in a few hours she had added thirty new words to her vocabulary. (Keller, *The Story of My Life,* p. 316)

What stands out in both of the above quotations, but especially in Cassirer's analysis, is the overly intellectual character of the treatment of the event. To speak of what happened to Helen Keller in terms of levels of "inner attitudes," "consciousness," "symbolic representation," and epistemic "distance" is to buy into a way of thinking about this pivotal event that begs all the important questions. Even Sullivan's penchant for construing words as "names" for "things" tends to obscure the truly significant facts contained in her own report.

What is crucial to note in Helen Keller's achievement is that it was just that, an achievement! That is to say, it was something she did as a unitary, embodied consciousness. Thus, her new level of human activity grew out of and continued to manifest itself in her bodily skills and behavior patterns. Moreover, it is misleading to speak as if she came to understand that symbols represent objects, since this casts the whole experience in terms of propositional knowledge. What happened, rather, was that she went from not being able to use, or simply not using, linguistic symbols to being able to use them. In short, Helen Keller's new "knowledge" was more a knowledge of how to do something than it was a knowledge that something is the case.

Equally as important, and equally overlooked in nearly all accounts, is the obvious fact that this momentous experience took place in a concrete, task-oriented context. Although there had been a month of training in sign language, including many practice sessions aimed at precisely this sort of breakthrough, the great event itself did not occur in a practice session. Helen Keller had spilled the water in an act of disobedience, and Annie Sullivan was disciplining her by making her refill the pitcher at the pumphouse. Being the extraordinary teacher that she was, she faithfully once again signed the word w-a-t-e-r into Keller's hand.

In other words, while she was engaged in a specific task in cooperation with another person, Helen Keller came to understand the relation between signs and the world. But as Wittgenstein would point out, the word "understand" does not here indicate some private "inner awareness" that floated across Keller's consciousness. Rather, it signifies that she had acquired the ability to use language to achieve certain ends in her physical and social environment. In and through the act of accomplishing one task with certain tools, she discovered the possibility of using symbolization itself as a tool.

The "ostensive definitions" provided by Sullivan whenever she finger-spelled into Keller's hand while putting her in physical contact with some feature of the world around her were not understood as being exemplars of a general activity, namely, signifying, as well as a particular association established between certain tactile patterns and specific features of the environment. As J. L. Austin might have put it, by signing individual symbols into Keller's hand, Sullivan was both saying something and showing how something could get said. It is this supervenient or piggyback relationship between the locutionary force and the illocutionary force of Sullivan's "pointing" activity that Keller came to understand.

The difficulty would seem to be, as Wittgenstein so clearly pointed out, that the activity of giving ostensive definitions is itself so fundamental that it cannot be taught by ostensive definition; one cannot teach it by pointing at it! In other words, a seemingly unfathomable mystery surrounds the task of enabling a prelinguistic child to participate in language, since at the primordial level linguistic activity is not reducible to other types of activity. There would seem to be no way to get from square zero to square one. The fact is, however, that this mystery, while not susceptible to intellectual explanation, is resolved quite well at the activity level. Children, including Helen Keller, learn to speak by being spoken to in concrete contexts as if they understand, and they do not if they are not!

The secret lies, it seems, in our ability to grasp and incorporate two activities in one, to participate in and thus understand one process in and through another. Wittgenstein puzzled over the seeming impossibility of teaching a child how to use—how to understand!— relative pronouns such as "here," "there," "this," and "that," since their meaning is supervenient on their use in context. We point by means of these terms; we cannot point at them except by using them and trusting that children will catch on to the fact that we are doing two things at once, namely, pointing at objects or places and showing how and that we can point at such things. This process is an excellent paradigm, or metonymy, of the larger question concerning the acquisition of language in general. All we can do is use language with and around preliterate children in the everyday activities of life, trusting that they will imitate us at one level and thereby come to participate with us at another level of this singular activity we call speech.

Once again it needs to be stressed that the sort of level of knowledge involved in language acquisition is clearly not to be understood as separate from other, prelinguistic and distinctively somatic activities, such as sound-play, gesturing, and imitation. All such activities are equally cognitive and equally somatic, even though some are more complex and mediated in nature. Even conceptual or propositional knowledge is an activity involving skills acquired through practice and participation with other practitioners. Moreover, it is only achieved by and while engaging in other, less complex and more physically direct activities. All knowing is a kind of doing.

Another thinker who has puzzled deeply and more fruitfully over the ramifications of Helen Keller's breakthrough is the highly acclaimed American novelist from Louisiana, Walker Percy. One of the themes, if not the dominating theme, of his fascinating collection of essays, *The Message in the Bottle,* is how to explicate these ramifications for a theory of how language works. He begins by postulating what he calls, in good Southern fashion, the "Delta Factor." He tries to fathom the Keller phenomenon in terms of the three-way relationship between a speaker, an object, and a symbol. Percy initially concluded that the "short-circuit" of the sequential stimulus-response pattern, which allowed Keller to become a member of the speaking community and which explains the origin and continuation of language in general, is an irreducible mystery. One is left with the account Keller herself gives of her experience:

> Someone was drawing water and my teacher placed my hand under the spout. As the cool stream gushed over one hand, she spelled into the other the word "water," first slowly then rapidly. I stood still, my whole attention fixed upon the motion of her fingers. Suddenly I felt a misty consciousness as of something forgotten—a thrill of returning thought; and somehow the mystery of language was revealed to me. I knew then that "w-a-t-e-r" meant the wonderful cool something that was flowing over my hand. That living word awakened my soul, gave it light, hope, joy, set it free! There were barriers still, it is true, but barriers that could in time be swept away. (Percy, pp. 34–35)

Later in his book Percy returns to the Keller phenomenon and offers a much more thorough treatment of it in relation to an overall theory of language and knowledge. Here he shifts from speaking of the three-way "Delta Factor" to employing a quadratic formula that better reveals the "tetradic structure" of the speech situation. The new dimension is supplied, unsurprisingly, by incorporating the hearer(s) into the model. Speech, after all, is directed at other persons, and the interaction between speaker and hearer is crucial to determining the actuality and significance of any communication. Percy makes a number of comments in which he acknowledges the fundamental role of social interaction in giving rise to language and meaning, specifically noting the contribution of G. H. Mead.

However, Percy does not think that the social dimension of linguistic activity can account for its specifically referential character, and it is with this that he is especially concerned. Moreover, he is particularly interested in the naming relationship between words and the world. Exactly what does it mean, as Helen Keller herself put it, to "know that w-a-t-e-r means that wonderful cool something flowing over" one's hand? This is how Percy finally resolves the issue:

> In its essence the making and the receiving of the naming act consist in a coupling, an apposing of two real entities, the uttered name and the object. It is this pairing which is unique and unprecedented in the causal nexus of significatory meaning. But what is the nature of this pairing? The two terms, it is clear, are related in some sense of identification, yet not a real identity. . . . Helen knows the water through and by means of the symbol. (p. 261)

This way of putting the matter is, indeed, helpful. The mediational character of language is focused in terms of the concept of intentionality, which has roots in both scholastic and phenomenological philosophy. The "meaning of meaning" can only be grasped in and through participating in linguistic activity, the general notion of meaning being supervenient on particular uses of language. All of this fits nicely with the suggestions made earlier about enabling a prelinguistic child to develop the skill of doing two things at the same time, the one by means of the other. Nevertheless, there are at least two additional features of linguistic activity that need to be developed more fully.

One is the social character of speech. What is missing in Percy's account is any treatment of the relation between the speaking community and the tasks they have in common. Of course the semantic or denotative dimension of language is not going to arise simply out of a consideration of speaker-bearer relationship, but people do not interrelate in a vacuum. People speak and respond to one another in concrete physical circumstances in order to accomplish specific undertakings and fulfill particular needs. It is this environmental and contextual dimension that provides a more complete understanding of the referential function of language. People do not just "refer to" or "name" things in the world; they do so pragmatically, for the attainment of certain ends. Thus, any account of the denotative function of language that fails to take up the task-centered quality of speech will end up in a cul-de-sac. Helen Keller came to "understand" how language works, neither by being told about it, thinking about it, nor by simply repeating verbal patterns endlessly. Rather, she achieved her breakthrough in the process of a real-life situation; she encountered language in use in her own circumstances and incorporated it into her own repertoire of skills. Again, to know is to do.

A second thing missing from Percy's account of how language is acquired is acknowledgment of the crucial role played by participation on the part of learner. His treatment, like that of Cassirer, of Helen Keller's accomplishment is in the final analysis still too intellectualist and passive to provide us with a significant insight. The great leap that Keller made—the leap all users of language must make—did not arise in a conceptual vacuum, devoid of embodied, behavioral activity. The "short-circuit" of sequential stimulus-response patterning that Percy speaks of does not just happen; it is not a miracle in which speech springs full-blown from the mind.

Rather, Helen Keller had been drawn by Annie Sullivan into participation in the everyday activities of human life along with and by means of the common and corporate activity of speech. Language cannot be learned apart from involvement with the world, nor can the world of human beings be understood apart from involvement with language. Helen Keller's grasping of language occurred as a result of her being continually immersed in it in conjunction with her involvement in the world around her.

Initially, this participation took the form of simple imitation. It then evolved to obedience and recitation. Finally, in the midst of a specific setting and task, these lower-level skills were transformed, as if—but not—by magic, into the more complex and comprehensive skills of using language to get things done. While engaged in the familiar activities of signing and touching, Helen Keller at last understood that these activities were not ends in themselves but mere means to a broader end, that of communication. In and through her participation in one level or form of linguistic activity, Keller began to participate at yet another, higher level. She understood that we can do more than one thing at once with symbols, whether tactile or oral.

Helen Keller's discovery was highly dramatized by the once-and-for-all quality it bore because of her relatively advanced age of five, but it was in essence no different from the participatory process all members of the speaking community go through. Think of how prelinguistic children sitting at the dinner table thrust themselves into the general conversation with oral outbursts whenever the volume of

the talking and laughing rises beyond normal. The children experience noisemaking as an end in itself, and they want to be part of the
action. Consider how they "talk" on play telephones long before they
have any vocabulary or with "words" they have made up. They have
learned the major speech-act intonations and thus go along asking
questions, giving orders, telling and laughing at jokes, and so on, all
as ends in themselves. When they learn to do things in the real world
with these utterances, when they know how to use them as means to
other ends, then they, like Helen Keller, have come to understand language. Throughout this process, there is no substitute for embodied
participation. Doing leads to and constitutes knowing.

Merleau-Ponty, Polanyi, and Helen Keller

By this day the main themes of Wittgenstein's later work are common knowledge. He has invited us to look at language not as one-
dimensional but as an open-ended medium for accomplishing specific tasks in concrete contexts. He has suggested that the primary
unit of signification is not the individual, isolated utterance but the
broader context of social activity within which an utterance is used,
what he termed the "language-game." The relationships among these
language-games overlap and crisscross each other in exceedingly
complex and fascinating ways, giving rise to linguistic modification
and innovation on the one hand and provoking and bewitching those
who study language on the other hand. These language-games find
their common ground and justification in the human "form of life,"
the behavior patterns that characterize our shared way of being-in-
the-world. Language and action are inextricably woven together to
form the fabric that constitutes both our prehension and our knowledge of the world.

These are familiar enough notions with respect to the question of
the nature of language, but rarely are they explored in relation to the
issues surrounding the problem of the acquisition of language. The
base camp for such explorations must be the fundamental Wittgensteinian insight that language is, after all, an activity-centered phenomenon. It is not comprised of isolated statements standing alone
or joined together in static inferential sequences of a deductive or
inductive nature. Rather, language arises in social contexts where

speakers, as persons engaged in intentional and complex activity, seek to accomplish certain tasks. In this sense, language can be thought of as a tool, and meaning can be seen as a function of use.

One important ramification of this radical shift in our understanding of language is the seemingly obvious fact that children acquire their mother tongue in the everyday push-and-pull of task-oriented human life. They are not given certain words to learn, along with specific definitions (whether lexical or ostensive), and thereby initiated into the speaking community. On the contrary, from the very first day — or before!—they are spoken to as if they were already members of the linguistic community. In spite of the fact that they do not understand a single word or sound, tiny infants are addressed, questioned, and responded to as if they did understand. And it is only because they are spoken to in this way that they come to participate in language at all.

It is often argued that the bedrock from which language builds, and thus the best explanation of how speakers get from square zero to square one in acquiring language, is ostensive definition. It is claimed that by means of pointing to, touching, or moving various aspects of reality, a speaker is able to convey the meanings of the words representing these aspects. However, Wittgenstein makes it clear that (1) we do not learn the meanings of individual words prior to learning the meanings of the sentences and, more importantly, the meaning of the language-games in which they are employed; (2) the act of pointing itself is part of a complex linguistic activity that cannot be learned by means of pointing; and (3) the meanings of such common terms as "here" and "there," and "now" and "then" can be learned only in situ because they are relative to the speaker's location in space and time and cannot be pointed at.

The mention of space and time serves as a useful transition to a brief consideration of the main ideas of Maurice Merleau-Ponty as they bear on the question of language acquisition. The fulcrum of Merleau-Ponty's phenomenological treatment of the human way of being-in-the-world is the notion of embodiment. After offering a systematic critique of both empiricist and rationalist accounts of perception and understanding, Merleau-Ponty posits the body as the axis of all human experience and knowledge. He contends that it is only in and through our bodily mobility and interaction with other physical objects and human bodies that we both structure our world and come to know it. The world is not observed passively, as a static framework; rather, it is encountered, geared into, and woven by means of our reaching out for and participating in it.

Our induction into language follows a similar pattern. Merleau-Ponty agrees with Wittgenstein that language must be understood as a dimension or mode of behavior, not in the Skinnerian sense but in the pragmatist sense of getting jobs done in social reality. Just as our bodies serve as the axis of our interaction with the physical world, so our speech functions as the pivot point of our existence in relation to other persons. Moreover, Merleau-Ponty even stresses the Wittgensteinian theme that our language does not represent thought but expresses it, or "accomplishes" it. [Language is viewed as an extension of our embodied existence, for not only is it impossible without a body, but it frequently serves as a way of altering the environment (getting the door closed, making agreements, evoking feelings, and so on).]

Meaning, according to Merleau-Ponty, is mediated in and through our speech-acts and their accompanying embodied behavior. It is not deduced or constructed from linguistic symbols, as from some pre-established code system. Children do not first establish that adults are speaking a language and then set about discovering how it works, as we generally do when we learn a second language. Meaning is neither read off nor read into language but is *encountered in* it. Both of these stressed words are important. Meaning is "encountered" in the sense that we are engaged by it rather than merely exposed to it. And we encounter it "in" language because while it is more than vocabulary and syntax (is "transcendent" to them), it cannot be grasped apart from them (is "imminent" in them).

Merleau-Ponty affirms and argues that we come into the world as "meaning-seeking" beings. In our bodies we reach out for significance; we do not wait for it to confront us. We wriggle, twist, grasp, suck, and kick by way of discovering and interacting with our physical environment. Tiny infants have been shown to be able to distinguish real human faces from pretend ones (and their mother's from those of other persons, as well) and to be able to imitate their mother's act of sticking out her tongue. In like manner, we come into the world seeking symbolic significance. We make sounds, listen for them, imitate them, experiment with them, and even invent them from the very outset. Speech, as an extension or mode of our bodily form of life, is our way of moving around in "social space," which is, along with physical space, a complimentary dimension of the world rather than a separate domain.

For Merleau-Ponty, speech, as well as bodily activity, is to be understood in terms of the notion of intentionality. Our consciousness is not only always consciousness of something, but our reality is both constituted and experienced as meaningful. Thus, we both act and speak in the world as intentional beings, as persons who expect, find, and create meaning and significance through interaction with other embodied persons in spatial and historical contexts. It is this fabric of intentionality into which children are born, and they acquire language by being woven into it by those who are already part of it. Neither mere exposure nor simply intellectual capacity can account for this phenomenon. Embodied social interaction, as anticipated, expected, and participated in, forms the matrix from within which language arises.

There are two specific aspects of language that Merleau-Ponty singles out as especially crucial to this acquisition process. The first is onomatopoeia and the second is gestural meaning. There is an actual physical connection between language and the world in the former instance, all the way from imitating nonhuman sounds in the environment to exploiting the tone of such words as "hiss," "kick," "smooth," "babble," and their counterparts in other natural languages. In the case of gestural meaning, the use of facial expressions, bodily gestures, and tone of voice are an integral part of the meaningful gestalt of context. Children interact with these so-called nonlinguistic features of the communication process as much as with the symbol system. Apart from an encounter with these features, a child could not be able to acquire language.

It should be clear by now how all of this applies with special significance to Helen Keller's breakthrough. It did not "just happen" but grew out of her embodied interaction with her physical environment on the one hand and with Annie Sullivan on the other. More specifically, she was brought into the human use of language at the invitation and insistence of one member of the speaking community in the process of accomplishing various real-life projects. In addition, all of this was possible because Helen Keller came equipped, as nearly all of us do, with a "meaning-seeking" drive and the capacities necessary to its fulfillment. In her case the tactile and gestural aspects of speech were particularly, though not uniquely, focused.

Finally, let us turn to the work of Michael Polanyi for a cognitive schema that both coordinates many of the foregoing emphases and provides some fundamental insights of its own. There are two major thrusts in Polanyi's epistemological investigations; the one concerns the legitimacy of tacit knowing, and the other its primacy. After briefly sketching out these two themes, I shall bring them to bear directly on the question of language acquisition.

Polanyi proposes that we view the cognitive dimension of human experience as comprised of a continuum between two poles, that of explicit knowing and that of tacit knowing. The former arises out of the interaction between focal awareness and conceptual activity. When our attention is focused on discrete aspects or features of our sociophysical environment and we construe them in terms of intellectual categories—as data, concepts, inferences, theories, and the like— then we can be said to be engaged in explicit knowing. Herein we seek to be as analytic, precise, logical, and objective as possible, and we recognize as knowledge only that which can be articulated and defended. These concerns have become the hallmark of cognitive responsibility in the West and have proven their value by enabling us to ferret out superstition, authoritarianism, and all manner of conceptual confusions.

Tacit knowing arises out of the interaction between what Polanyi calls "subsidiary awareness" and bodily activity. All focal awareness is grounded in and only makes sense against the backdrop of subsidiary or subliminal awareness. For example, the reader is focally aware of the meaning of the sentences here written while being only subsidiarily aware of the specific terms and grammatical structures being used. In other words, our awareness has a "from-to," or vectorial, structure; that is, in order to attend *to* anything at all in a focal sense, we must be able to attend *from* other things in a subsidiary sense. When our bodily activity engages or is engaged by these subsidiary features, when we, in short, make physical judgments about various aspects of our world (whether about the location of the coffee table when walking through a dark living room, or the trajectory of a fly ball we are supposed to catch, or the meaning of an unfamiliar sound in the next room), we participate in and exhibit what Polanyi calls "tacit knowing."

This tacit dimension of our cognitive experience is not characterized in the same way as the explicit dimension. Rather, it is rooted in what Polanyi calls "indwelling," the process by means of which we immerse ourselves in the subsidiary features of surroundings, through bodily interaction, and by means of which they become extensions of our own agency in the world. The meaning-gestalts that are formed by means of our indwelling certain features of our own environment are the result of an integrative act. The logic of an integrative act, unlike that of an inferential process, is irreversible in the sense that once closure is reached, the prehender cannot return to the epistemic position he or she was in before closure was reached. It's the difference between retracing the steps of a syllogistic argument and trying not to see a puzzle-picture once you have "seen" it.

A simple example of tacit knowing in which indwelling and integrative acts are clearly present is that of learning to drive a stick-shift automobile. One attends from the coordination level already achieved in one's body (an exceedingly complex level, it should be noted) to specific tasks of manipulating features of the immediate environment, which are initially experienced as isolated realities, by way of incorporating them into an integrated, meaningful whole. At each successive stage of integration, what were isolated tasks, and received our focal attention, become woven into a larger whole from which we attend as we attend to the next to incorporate it into the whole. Clutch, accelerator, gearshift, and steering wheel all must be integrated into a single activity that we call "driving the car." The key to this process of integration is not that of explicit knowing, of precise definition and conceptual formulation, but rather, a function of participation, of indwelling. There is no substitute, as with swimming and other activities, for simply engaging in the activity of driving itself, "pretending," as it were, that we are driving until we find that we are. And once we know how to drive, we cannot reverse the process and begin again as if we did not know how to do it.

Coming to know another person, finding your way around in a large city — or forest — feeling your way into a new field of study are all examples of tacit knowing at a much more complex level. In each case we bring who we are and what we already know into a diffused field of unknown particulars. Through our participatory interaction (indwelling) with these particulars at a subsidiary level of awareness, they are incorporated into our meaning constellations through integrative acts and thus become part of the fulcrum for our continued explorations and acquisitions.

This brings us to the second main thrust of Polanyi's work, namely, the more radical notion that tacit knowledge is not only legitimate but in fact primordial. Polanyi argues most cogently that all explicit knowing is and must be grounded in tacit knowing, since the former is dependent, both logically and experientially, on a context and a vectorial perspective that can only be supplied by a prior and conceptually different epistemological footing. It is only by relying on unarticulated factors that we can articulate others, whether we are dealing with meanings or reasonings. Moreover, at the deepest level, our common commitment (what Polanyi calls "universal intent") to the activity of acquiring knowledge about ourselves and the world, and to communicating that knowledge, can itself be neither fully articulated nor substantiated. At the primordial level, our cognitive and valuational activities are symbiotic, and all of our cognitive and valuational activities at the explicit conceptual level are dependent thereon.

To return to the question of the acquisition of language, from a Polanyian perspective it seems clear that children, beginning as newborn infants, are immersed in the medium of language even as they come to exist in and breathe oxygen. They come to indwell social reality through their "enlanguagement" in much the same way that they come to indwell physical reality through embodiment. At first this immersion is strictly a form of physical behavior within a diffuse, undifferentiated sea of sounds and accompanying activity. Certain integrative acts occur that in turn provide an axis around and by means of which further meaning closures begin to form. From this tacit base a child moves toward explicit articulation in speech, at first in terms of requests, responses, names, and questions, then in terms of declaration, inventions, puns, and conversation, and later in terms of concepts, rules, and reasonings.

The crucial factor in a Polanyian treatment of language acquisition is the notion of tacit knowing as rooted in subsidiary awareness and bodily activity and as providing the fulcrum for all explicit knowing. The empiricist or behaviorist account emphasizes mere exposure and physical response, failing to incorporate either the subsidiary character of the child's linguistic awareness or the embodied intentionality of the speaking community. The rationalist or structuralist account emphasizes the equipment or capacities with which the child encounters linguistic reality but neglects both the crucial role of bodily activity as the matrix of linguistic meaning and the task-centered orientation of the speaking community. Thus Polanyi's schema provides a way of incorporating the strengths while avoiding the weaknesses of these two main yet conflicting schools of thought.

Polanyi has constructed an epistemological perspective that grounds cognition itself in our embodied existence, thereby shedding a great deal of light on the role of embodiment in language acquisition. To return to our original way of putting the issue, the explanation of how we got from square zero, as nonlinguistic beings, to square one of the linguistic community is to be found in those tacit, integrative acts that result from our bodily awareness (both verbal and nonverbal) of the social community into which we are born, acts that result in our ability to focus specific linguistic patterns and tasks and to thereby participate in that same community.

To stress exposure and reinforcement, à la Skinner, is not sufficient. Nor is stressing the structure of the human mind, à la Chomsky. What is needed is an emphasis on the dynamic interaction between such factors at the intersection of intentional embodiment (following Merleau-Ponty) on the one hand and task-centered, social interaction (following Wittgenstein) on the other. The child comes into the world with certain capacities and expectations, tasks and commitments. The two indwell each other through their mutual embodiment, both linguistic and nonlinguistic, and the child forms and builds on certain integrative acts that provide both its entry point into and its leverage point within the linguistic dimension of existence.

The implications of the foregoing distinctions for an understanding of Helen Keller's achievement should be clear. Her induction into the speaking community, as in all cases, was not accomplished by explicit instruction but by subsidiary and bodily interaction with her sociophysical environment. By means of the embodied indwelling of the things and persons around her, along with the finger-spelling routines, Keller performed an integrative act in which these particulars came together as a comprehensive whole, not unlike what is involved in learning to drive a stick-shift car. By "pretending" to talk she became a talker, in much the same way that by pretending to swim we become swimmers. As before, to know is to do.

4

Autism and Language Acquisition

Autism provides another example of a person existing on the threshold of language, one that is quite different from those cases we have considered thus far. An autistic child seemingly withdraws into his or her own world by essentially ignoring other people and refusing to enter into language. This phenomenon is of special interest because it involves what appears to be a willful *choice* not to speak. Because there remains a great deal to be understood about this puzzling and tragic behavioral pattern, there has been little, if any, progress toward a remedy. In this light it is especially interesting to consider the account given by Barry and Samahria Kaufman of their successful struggle to bring their son Raun out of autism. Our focus will be on those aspects of their account that bear directly on the process of language acquisition. The gripping and highly instructive story is found in the Kaufmans' book, *Son Rise: The Miracle Continues.*

Raun's Story

When Raun Kaufman was four weeks old, he suddenly developed a severe ear infection. The antibiotics he received soon caused serious dehydration and Raun was placed in a pediatric intensive-care unit. After five days the fever broke and Raun was on his way to full recovery, but not without serious damage to both of his eardrums. Although it was clearly possible that his hearing would be impaired, the first year of Raun's life gave no indication of any impairment. In fact, throughout his first year Raun showed every sign of developing into an extremely alert and lively child.

However, when he was about one year old, his parents began to notice increasing audio insensitivity. He responded less and less to his name and to general sounds, becoming increasingly aloof, as if some internal voice was distracting his attention away from what was going on around him. Over the next four months he began to stare off into space for long periods of time and became increasingly passive toward his immediate environment. Finally, even his prelinguistic pointing and gesturing ceased, leaving Raun completely mute. At the same time, testing indicated that he was not deaf.

The Kaufmans frantically searched for some explanation for what was happening to their son. After reading a number of books, they reluctantly came to the conclusion that he was suffering from autism. Their description of this collection of loosely associated symptoms reads: "Antisocial and aloof patterns of activity; hypnotic preoccupation with spinning, rocking and other repetitive movements; a lack of verbal communication; a tendency to look through people; a fascination with inanimate objects; seemingly deaf, unresponsive, and rejection of physical contact" (p. 21).

The most well-known research at that time had been done by Bruno Bettelheim and presented in his book *The Empty Fortress.* The vast majority of the autistic children Bettelheim studied were hospitalized or consigned to custodial care for the rest of their lives; their personalities disintegrated, and their families often fell apart as well. Bettelheim generally blamed the parents of these children, especially the mothers, for being excessively "cold" and thereby triggering their children's autistic withdrawal. The Kaufmans were deeply perplexed by this judgmental explanation, since they themselves knew that their personalities and home life were anything but cold and unresponsive.

The Kaufmans sought professional advice from various clinics that had been established to treat autistic children. In every case the people who ran these clinics were extremely pessimistic at best, indicating that in their view autism was essentially incurable, or they were downright uncooperative at worst, saying that Raun was much too young for them to be of any help. Through the Autism Society of America, the Kaufmans met parents of other autistic children, nearly all of whom appeared to have given up looking for a cure for their children's illness. The various schools the Kaufmans contacted offered severe behavioral modification training as a means of helping parents control their children's often unruly behavior, but no one held out any hope for or means of effecting anything like a cure.

Because the Kaufmans believed both in their own love for Raun and in his potential for developing into a normal child, they refused to give in to the pessimism that surrounded them. Having already been exposed to the teachings of what is called humanistic psychology, they began to consider the possibility of trying to help Raun on their own by means of these teachings. The two basic principles upon which they decided to proceed were (1) total commitment to creating a nonjudgmental environment for Raun and (2) an all-out effort to show their acceptance of him by imitating his behavior, rather than demanding that he learn to imitate theirs. In short, the Kaufmans decided to try to enter into Raun's private, inner world through imitation and acceptance of it, instead of requiring him to participate in their own public, outer world. Barry Kaufman articulates their program in these words:

> We initiated a very elaborate imitation format that extended beyond our periods of observation. When Raun spun plates for hours at a time in a room, Samahria and I and whoever else was in the house gathered up plates and pans and spun beside him. Sometimes as many as seven of us spun with him, turning his "isms" into an acceptable, joyful and communal event. It was our way of being with him, of somehow demonstrating to him that he was okay, that we loved him, that we cared, and that we accepted him wherever he was. (p. 49)

This radical methodology represents nearly the exact opposite of the standard behavioral modification approach that is commonly used to control, not cure, autism. In this latter methodology a great deal of negative reinforcement is used, since autistic children do not often engage in behavior that can be reinforced positively. Thus such techniques as yelling, pinching, and slapping, as well as squirting in the face with squirt guns, locking in closets, and even electric shocks, have become standard practice in "treating" autistic children. The message that gets sent by such methods is one that tells the children that what they do, and even who they are, is essentially unacceptable.

Raun was seventeen months old when his parents began their program in earnest. Twelve hours a day, day in and day out, for many weeks they followed and participated in his every activity, spinning, rocking, and flapping their fingers for hours on end. Along the way they made copious notes, jotting down their observations of anything that seemed significant in Raun's behavior. One important event was described in this manner:

It happened during the second week of our marathon observation period. He had spun every round object he could find on the kitchen floor. . . . But this one time he came upon a rectangular shoe box. He picked it off the floor and held it in his hands for almost twenty five minutes. He did not move, except to occasionally stroke the cardboard with his fingers, while moving his gaze back and forth along the edges of the box. Then quite suddenly he put the top of one of the corners of the box on the floor, balanced it firmly with his left hand and set it expertly in motion with his right. No trial and error. No practice run. He had actually used his mind analytically and with great sophistication in order to create the movement he had wanted . . . still only seventeen months old. (p. 54)

Raun continued to display his amazing manual dexterity, but consistently ignored the world of people and social interaction. The Kaufmans hypothesized that Raun found the world around him, including all moving physical objects, to be too confusing and threatening to become involved with, and thus he limited his interaction to those objects that he could control and manipulate when and as he wished. This would account for his refusal to participate in speech and for his inability to score above thirty on intelligence tests.

In order to better control Raun's environmental input, the Kaufmans moved their training sessions into the bathroom, which was monochromatic, quiet, and relatively simple in furnishings. Here Raun was especially fascinated with the fluorescent lights, and Samahria sought to imitate his staring at them while rocking back and forth in an effort to experience his inner world the way he did. She soon found that this behavior had a soothing and hypnotic effect even on her. It was easy to see how focusing in this way would enable one to shut out the outside world and thereby gain inner peace. Throughout these early days, Raun gave no indication of being aware that his mother was present.

However, "On the eleventh day, after spinning with him for over two full hours, Samahria noted a single casual sideward glance at her. She acknowledged and softly cheered his action" (p. 66). From this time on, Raun began to emerge from his private world, ever so slowly and cautiously, but steadily. Gradually he began to accept and even seek physical contact, to broaden the range of his attention and activities. His mother took great care to always remain at Raun's level, seeking eye contact, and she began to experiment with a wide variety of simple games and sensory explorations, trying to draw Raun into even minimal interaction. He did register fascination with most of her antics and experiments.

Raun showed increasing interest in food and became extremely responsive to music, even to the extent of seeking to coordinate his movements to it. Moreover, he engaged in more and more side glances to all the members of the family, especially his mother. All the while, of course, he continued to spin plates, to rock back and forth, and to flap his fingers. His parents continued to imitate him in these activities. Raun's older sisters were eager to participate in his training program, and they proved to be of considerable help, if only in releasing their parents from the pressure of the rigorous daily responsibility.

> One of the Kaufmans' goals was to show Raun that with minimal effort he could effect change and exert some control over the external world. At the dinner table, when he shook his head wildly back and forth, we all did the same with him. When he smiled, we all smiled back at him. If he stuck out his tongue, we all stuck our tongues out. Each time he watched us with fascination and delight. Sometimes he smiled. Other times he would quietly regard our behavior, becoming more and more aware that he could set the pace. (p. 81)

Another crucial step in Raun's growth toward "reentry" occurred when for the first time he became captivated by his own image in the mirror. After surveying his image cautiously, he moved back and forth to the right and to the left; then he went directly up to the image and touched it, nose to nose. Next, he moved out of the path of the mirror, then peeked back around its edge, only to encounter his own face once again. "Suddenly he emitted a wild, unfamiliar shout—a cry of incredible excitement and joy. He began to grunt and laugh with elation. Raun Kahlil had discovered himself" (p. 95). Raun continued to play with his newfound self in the mirror for twenty minutes, sticking out his tongue, shaking his head, jumping up and down, laughing and babbling softly, and touching his image with nearly every part of his body.

This encounter with himself in his mirror image triggered a new level of physical activity and motor skills in Raun. He soon began to play more spontaneously and diversely with his family members and even eventually with other children he met at the park. He also came to initiate crying as a way of indicating his wants. He even waved once to his father, or so it seemed.

Early on, Raun's father had tried one of Jean Piaget's experiments with a cookie in order to see if Raun could "reason" his way to a cookie that had been covered up with a newspaper right before his eyes. He had not been able to do it. The cookie seemed simply to go out of existence when it was removed from view. In the eleventh week of their program, Barry Kaufman tried this experiment again. This time Raun went to the newspaper, slid it aside, and ate the cookie. Then he proceeded to find and devour a large number of cookies that his father commenced to hide under various things all over the living room. The next day Raun actually put a picture puzzle together all by himself, a feat he had never even come close to accomplishing before. He was now about nineteen months old and had been involved in this experimental training for less than three months.

Although there was steady progress in Raun's development, there were also periods and episodes of regression, some clearly borne out of specific frustrations and others arising inexplicably. At about twenty months of age, he seemed to be withdrawing once again, so the Kaufmans eased up on their program and actually reverted, with Raun, to their initial imitative practices. Somehow this move seemed to allow him opportunity to rest and center himself, for soon he was his old "new," growing self again. He suffered another setback when his parents went away for the weekend, leaving him with a friend whom he knew well and liked. Raun went on a rampage of overturning furniture all over the house. Vickie, the friend, somewhat at a loss for what to do, joined in the "game" with Raun. Together they overturned nearly every piece of furniture in the house before they collapsed together on the floor, totally exhausted. Instead of retreating into his private world, Raun continued in the relationship with his baby-sitter, waiting for his parents to return. Throughout this episode he frequently called out for his "Mommy" and his "Daddy." When they returned, he was elated and continued on with his progress. The significance of this event lay in the fact that Raun had, in a crisis, chosen people over his former protective behavior. When he was twenty-four months old, after thirty weeks of the Kaufmans' special training program, Raun was tested once again at the same diagnostic facility he had been earlier. He talked, drew pictures, interacted with people, and accurately named nearly every object in the room, including its color. The doctors at the clinic had extreme difficulty believing that this was the same child they had examined several months earlier. In over half of the tests Raun functioned at the thirty- to thirty-six-month level. Over the next months and early childhood years, Raun continued to develop rapidly.

Two areas in which Raun actually came to excel were mathematics and music. When he reached six years of age, he entered first grade and continued as an outstanding student and likable person. He graduated from high school at the top of his class and is now doing well in college.

The Kaufmans' Techniques

The foregoing account of the Kaufmans' successful efforts leads directly to a consideration of the particulars of their method, namely, imitation. Specifically, we are especially interested in the relation between this imitative technique and Raun's acquisition of language.

Out of their commitment to affirm Raun as a person by striving to be as accepting and nonjudgmental as possible, the Kaufmans began to pay closer attention to his peculiar behavioral patterns, such as rocking back and forth, flapping his fingers, and spinning plates. Feeling quite frustrated over being unable to communicate with Raun and having nothing to do other than observe him, they began to enter into his behavior as a kind of "game."

> We started to imitate him—for him, but also for us, hoping in this way to find some relevant insight or understanding. We also believed that imitating him was one of the few channels open to us through which we could let him know that we were with him. We wanted to pick up on his case in order to communicate with him. If he couldn't follow us, we wanted to follow him. (p. 49)

As mentioned previously, during the early days of this experiment Raun continued to seem unaware of his parents' presence and imitation of his actions, living in his own private world. However, on the eleventh day his mother noticed Raun make a single sideward glance toward her, seemingly acknowledging an awareness of her presence as a participant in his intense, compulsive behavior. This was perhaps the first point of real contact between Raun and his mother since the onset of his sickness and subsequent withdrawal. This point of contact led to Raun's acceptance of increased bodily interaction between them. From here on there was steady, though occasionally regressive, development in Raun's journey out of his private world.

In addition, this initial establishment of eye contact became the catalyst for increased efforts on the part of the Kaufmans to reach Raun by creating contexts within which he would be stimulated and encouraged to make eye contact with them. Mealtime turned out to be an excellent opportunity for such interaction, since his mother could remain at eye level with Raun while both speaking to him and feeding him with a spoon. They found that soon Raun would look past the food as it approached his mouth and directly into their eyes, if only for an instant. Raun also seemed interested in, and even a bit fascinated with, some of the other playful antics his mother devised by way of capturing his attention during routine, everyday activities. Thus imitation, theirs of him, led to the beginnings of a two-way line of communication between Raun and his parents.

Although this imitative technique on the part of the Kaufmans did produce these early results of initial eye contact and increased attention span, Raun remained essentially inert when it came to the initiation of any bodily contact or socially induced activity. He did learn to stand in front of the tape recorder in order to get his mother to turn it on so that he could listen to the music he had come to enjoy. Nevertheless, he never made any other effort to indicate intentions or responses to what was going on around him. More specifically, in Barry Kaufman's words, he engaged in "no prelinguistic language — no pointing or gestures to indicate desires" (p. 74).

As previously described, the family's imitative behavior extended to Raun's seemingly random facial movements at the dinner table. This sort of inclusion, of being drawn into interactive relationship with others on the basis of his own behavior, clearly seemed to be effective with Raun. Also, Raun's encounter with his own image in the mirror in a way constitutes yet another instance of being drawn into interactive behavior through being imitated, albeit by his own reflection. A parallel instance to that of imitating his facial movements took place when Raun, again at the dinner table, began banging his fork on the table and making a loud humming noise. As the rest of the family joined in this spontaneous "concert," with everyone banging and singing at the top of their lungs, Raun smiled broadly as he looked from one person to another, thoroughly enjoying being part of the group. The episode ended in a crescendo of laughter.

Raun's first move toward linguistic communication took the form of bodily movement in response to the mentioning of food. As Barry Kaufman puts it:

> Even though mute and without gestures (he never pointed), Raun began to recognize some words and expressions. When he heard the word food, he became alert immediately. . . . We had simplified our speech purposely, trying to make our words and their meanings more digestible. We named aloud every object and activity. In fact, we talked incessantly as a way to familiarize him with more humanistic and socialized interaction, which allowed us to give a more cognitive dimension to our presence. (p. 71)

An even more dramatic level of this bodily communication was reached on the day that Raun walked up to the refrigerator and started to cry. When his mother asked him if wanted some juice, he began to cry more loudly. He had actually indicated something he wanted; he had initiated an effort to communicate his needs. That same afternoon Raun stood before the closed door and began to cry. When the door was opened, he stopped crying and entered the room. A bit later he stood in front of the little gate at the foot of the stairs and cried once again. When the gate was opened, he quickly climbed the stairs and ceased crying. Kaufman observes: "He had moved into an active stage of prelinguistic communication. He wanted things external to himself and now actively tried to get them. . . . For the first time, he brought himself into our world and became an active initiating participant in our family unit" (p. 88).

During the same week Raun began to mimic words he heard his parents and siblings use, but although he consistently used the exact tone of voice and inflection they had used, he did not seem to grasp the significance of these utterances. He repeated the words in much the same way a parrot would, randomly and with no behavioral connection. One is reminded here of how Helen Keller first learned to sign the words her teacher was teaching her. She would sign the words completely out of context, even in her sleep, without any connection with each other or with the objects around her. Nevertheless, such mimicry constituted the first step on the complex road to linguistic communication in both cases.

Before long, Raun began taking his parents by the hand, pulling them toward objects he wanted, and crying. When he was given the object, Raun would stop crying. At nineteen months he was functioning at the appropriate level in terms of motor skills and activities, something of a miracle in itself. However, in terms of language and social skills, he was performing at the level of a nine-month-old child. This fact led the Kaufmans to design a shorthand system of speaking to Raun. They substituted one-syllable, one-word designations for the regular words for objects they had been using: "ba" for "bottle," "wa" for "water," and "ju" for "juice," for example. Thus equipped, they began to urge Raun to substitute these sounds for his crying. They sought to be both helpful and firm in insisting on them.

The difficulty involved in this fresh approach was powerfully exemplified one evening at a small dinner party given by the Kaufmans. Raun came into the room, took his father by the hand, and began pulling him. Upon being asked what he wanted, Raun began to pull even more vigorously and burst into tears. His father told him that he would come with him if he would tell him what he wanted. Although Barry Kaufman wanted very much to get up and go with his son, he realized that to do so would undermine their recent efforts to get Raun to use language instead of crying to express his wishes. After a while Raun became exhausted and, placing his head on his father's shoulder, allowed himself to be stroked and soothed.

However, once rested, Raun repeated his pulling and crying routine, followed by the rest period, five full times before he finally fell asleep at his father's feet. Barry Kaufman was sure that Raun understood what he wanted him to do but was simply unwilling to speak in this situation. Raun knew the simplified vocabulary for what he wanted but refused to use it. Crying was easier. This type of episode is familiar to anyone who has ever raised or taught children. Raun was following the normal developmental stages but was doing so in truncated fashion, much like Helen Keller, who collapsed these stages into roughly one month at the age of five.

Something like a crisis began to develop in the Kaufman household. Raun became increasingly frustrated under the pressure of being expected to participate in language. His crying fits became more frequent and forceful. Then one morning, while standing by the sink crying, Raun was finally given a glass of water by his mother. As he drank the water, he mother repeated over and over, "This is water, Raun, 'wa.' Say 'wa,' Raun." Later that day he returned to the sink and repeated the procedure. His mother repeatedly asked him to tell her what he wanted. "Suddenly, twitching his eyes as if he was harnessing all the strength and the power in him, Raun blasted a word through his vocal chords and filled the room with his clear and loud voice. The little boy, who the experts said would never talk in a meaningful way, shouted 'WA'" (p. 139).

Still later in the day, Raun repeated this routine, complete with the utterance of the word "wa." That night at dinner, when he was finished eating, he surprised everyone by saying "down." Before going to bed, Raun received a glass of juice from his mother, and when he had drunk it, he handed the glass to his mother and said "more." Finally, on the way upstairs he uttered the word "ba," the shorthand word for "bottle." Four words in one day, each used in the proper context in order to get a particular task accomplished. Again one is reminded of Helen Keller. Not only did she, like Raun, achieve her linguistic breakthrough in an episode involving water, but she, too, virtually gushed forth a torrent of words once she was able to fit language into the world around her.

Following this incredible episode, the Kaufmans initiated a series of simple games that combined many of the shorthand words they were teaching Raun with the act of touching various parts of his body. "Raun, touch your nose. Clap your hands now. Super! Can you point to your eyes? Eyes? Yes, eyes! Great, you did it. Okay, shake your head. Hey, watch me do it. Head. Shakes. Yes, that's it. You're the best!" (p. 143). Raun loved these games, and once his mother had modeled her request, he showed his great ability for mimicry. Along with these verbal activities, the Kaufmans increased Raun's physical activity as well and even joined with him in rough-and-tumble games, which included jumping, rolling on the ground, and tickling.

In spite of all this progress, there were still times of great difficulty and frustration in the months ahead. During the sixteenth week of the training program, Raun once again began to withdraw and become uncooperative, even quite unruly. And so once again the Kaufmans relaxed their schedule and established an all-accepting atmosphere. This sort of roller-coaster, on-again off-again behavior pattern repeated itself for several weeks, until about the twentieth week, or when Raun was just over two years of age.

Then one day Raun simply returned from his private world for good. He once again embraced his parents and began to laugh and mimic them when they initiated their little games. Moreover, he again began to use the words he knew, increasing his vocabulary to seventy-five in one week. Although he continued to struggle at times, as do all normal children, Raun's progress in the acquisition of his natural language had turned a crucial corner and there was no looking back from this point on.

After the traumatic furniture-overturning episode described earlier, Raun was tested at the clinic again. To the astonishment of the doctors who had tested him before, Raun excelled in nearly every category beyond his chronological age of two years. At one point in his interview, Raun displayed his verbal abilities by naming all the objects and their colors in the room. Over the next year he continued to grow linguistically in leaps and bounds. At the age of three and-a-half years, he mastered first and second grade reading texts and became an avid inventor of simple games. His imaginative powers were in full display throughout all of his many activities. The Kaufmans sought to stimulate his imagination through fantasy and storytelling. Raun created many stories of his own.

In considering all this exciting progress and these spectacular turning points, it is important not to lose sight of the single most significant factor running throughout the whole phenomenon, namely, the cruciality of the part played by imitative activity on the part of both Raun and his parents, but especially the latter. Raun learned to participate in the social world around him by imitating it, but only after his parents had first entered his world by imitating his peculiar behavior patterns. In this way they built a bridge for him to find his way into their world.

Some Theoretic Ramifications

There are several philosophical implications of the Kaufmans' successful efforts to bring their son Raun out of autism. Of course, it must be acknowledged that there are many unanswered questions about their methodology and about their results. Theirs was not a strictly scientific experiment. Nevertheless, it must be admitted that quite a number of specialists had judged Raun to be a hopeless case of autism and later were forced to admit that he had made an astonishing recovery. The account given by the Kaufmans of Raun's early behavior, together with his obvious above-average accomplishments in later years, clearly establishes that they had significant insight into autistic withdrawal and into its reversal.

The most remarkable aspect of the Kaufmans' achievement is certainly the idea of imitation. With respect to the acquisition of one's natural language, the conventional wisdom, at both the lay and the learned level, has generally stressed the importance of the child's imitation of the adult speakers constituting its immediate speaking community. This belief in the cruciality of imitation on the part of the learner, fostered largely by the behaviorism of B. F. Skinner, has continued to hold sway in spite of the conclusive criticism provided by Noam Chomsky in his pivotal review of Skinner's book *Verbal Behavior*. Chomsky showed that if imitation were all that was involved, a child would never be able to understand or form unfamiliar sentences.

More significantly, at least for our present purposes, it should be clear on a moment's reflection that if a child's acquiring of the native tongue were solely dependent on the process of being rewarded for imitating adult speakers, the child might never learn to speak at all. The simple fact is that adult speakers, especially those in an infant's early speaking community, essentially reward nearly everything the child utters. Appropriate and inappropriate utterances alike are generally greeted with a great deal of positive reinforcement. Such indiscriminate reinforcement would make it impossible for a child to learn which adult utterances were to be imitated and which not. In short, while learner imitation may well be necessary to the acquisition process, it can hardly be sufficient.

What the Kaufmans' work calls our attention to is the inevitable reciprocal character of imitative activity in language acquisition. In deciding to go in after their son rather than try to force him out into their world, they highlighted and demonstrated the fact that in the actual learning process there is an essential give-and-take between those who already speak and those acquiring speech. Language is, at bottom, a social, interactive reality. Even at birth we speak to an infant as if it will understand us, and if we do not do this, the child probably never will understand us or speak. In a word, the ability to acquire language is dependent on reciprocal participation in a process far more complex than that of mere imitation.

As the Kaufmans have shown, it is the imitation by adult speakers of the child's behavior that also plays a crucial role in inviting the child into the speaking community. By being willing to enter their son's world, they indicated their desire to have him enter theirs. Even though their initial entry into Raun's world through imitating his peculiar behavior was not linguistic in nature, it laid the groundwork for his eventual participation in language.

Anyone who has paid attention to the peculiar nature of early child hood speech patterns, including those of the proximate adult speakers, must acknowledge the reciprocity inherent in the imitative character of speech. Anthropological linguists have established that some form of "baby talk" is pretty much a universal phenomenon. When adults speak to small children, they change the tone as well as the vocabulary of their speech. Moreover, children frequently invent utterances of their own which find their way into the adult vocabulary. "Bubba" and "Sissy" as names for brothers and sisters are obvious examples. Nearly every family has acquired idiosyncratic words initially derived from the mistakes or creativity of its small children. Raun's adaptation of the shorthand vocabulary devised by his parents, such as the words "ba" and "wa," for example, serves to illustrate this phenomenon.

An example from my own parental experience, mentioned in chapter 1, may serve further to demonstrate and clarify this point. When spoon-feeding our young daughter her morning cereal, we would first blow on each spoonful in order to cool it down. We taught her to do the same by saying, "Blow, Jodie, blow." She would repeat, "Bluh, bluh." Soon we were asking her if she would like some "bluh" for breakfast, and she would respond, "Bluh." Before long, we were asking each other if we had enough bluh on hand, or if we should pick up some bluh at the store. Thus "bluh" became the family word for cereal.

Another example comes to mind. Whenever I first meet small children, I begin "talking" to them by making clicking noises. They respond immediately by making noises of their own or by imitating my sounds. Soon they branch out to making other noises and sounds, such as giving me the "raspberry" or rapidly moving a finger up and down over their lips or humming. The point is that such "vocabulary" is familiar to small children because they are at the experimental stage with sounds and noises. Thus when I, in effect, begin imitating them in their own "language," they generally respond enthusiastically. This type of reciprocal exchange establishes the sort of interaction that is necessary to the enculturation involved in language acquisition. Imitation is clearly a two-way street.

If we push this imitative reciprocity to a deeper level, we slide into what is generally regarded as "prelinguistic" behavior. The babbling of an infant is also imitated by its initial significant others. Far from being at best irrelevant and at worst a waste of time, such imitation establishes a vital point of contact between the infant and the adult speaker. This form of behavior parallels that of the Kaufmans' imitative activity vis-à-vis Raun's autistic rocking, spinning, and flapping. The imitative behavior of adult speakers serves to engage the attention, as well as the intentionality, of the infant or child. To change the image, such behavior stimulates or activates the consciousness and imagination of the potential speaker.

At a deeper somatic level, the actual gestures and mobility of the small child also provide the matrix or loom within which is woven the fabric of human speech. The Kaufmans instinctively understood this and thus incorporated as much physical contract as possible into their efforts to establish communication with Raun. Not only did they seek to hold and interact somatically as much as possible with him, but they incorporated exaggerated gestures into their speech patterns, actually acting out as much as possible what they were saying to Raun. Signing and game playing became a significant part of their symbolic interaction with Raun, thus providing the framework within which linguistic utterances took on meaning for him.

There are two dramatic examples of how this imitative interaction was operative at the somatic level in Raun's case. One is the incident when he displayed his frustration over his parents' absence by running through the house and overturning all the furniture. This was clearly a symbolic act, and his baby-sitter was able to interact with him on this somatic level of communication by joining in with him, by imitating his anger, thereby indicating that she understood and was willing to accept his expression of frustration. A two-way bridge was established by means of an adult imitating a child's symbolic, albeit prelinguistic, behavior.

The other example is Raun's encounter with his own image in the mirror. At some point every child experiences its first self-conscious confrontation with its own image in a mirror, after failing to have done so on many previous occasions. At whatever stage and for whatever reason, when this encounter takes place, it is a momentous event. What is of special interest in this case is that the image in the mirror actually functions as another child-person imitating the actions and antics of the child in question. More specifically, the extensive probing of this mirror image by engaging in a wide variety of random movements, as well as in a number of deliberate actions, results in imitative activity of a highly refined and articulate order. This, in turn, elicits further expression and articulation on the part of the child. In this regard Raun was no exception.

All of this serves to bring home the point that not only does language arise out of the matrix of physical interaction with the world around us, but even somatic interactions pivot on the fulcrum of imitative reciprocity. In and through the push-and-pull of physical interaction with the world and each other, accompanied by continuous and task-directed speech, we absorb meaning. Moreover, both of these dimensions of symbolic interaction, the physical and the semantic, depend upon the process of mutual imitation.

It is here that we can see the importance of games and fantasy in the so-called prelinguistic phase of the acquisition of speech. By means of the give-and-take of simple games and songs, as well as by the process of pretending, young children are drawn into imitative behavior and come to an understanding of linguistic meaning. The

Kaufmans' use of games and make-believe clearly underscores the importance of reciprocal activity as the nexus of imitation and thus of linguistic acquisitions as well.

In my own experience I can well recall how the ritual of singing an old cowboy song to my four-month-old daughter while getting her ready for bed every night established a solid line of expectation and communication between us. She even began to anticipate the parts of the chorus where I would make a clicking sound, so that when these parts came around, we would both laugh and squeal together. Even though she could not verbalize in any way, my daughter participated significantly in this ritual, thus making it genuinely reciprocal. As time went on, she was able to make the clicking sound herself, and eventually she was able to sing the whole song along with me.

It is of course true that the imitative process can only lead a potential participant to the water of understanding; it cannot make him or her drink thereof. The magic or mystery whereby imitation is transformed into cognition is not fully explained or removed by tracing the pattern of imitative activity. This is made evident by those cases wherein imitation is fully operative but understanding does not take place. A humorous example of such lack of understanding is seen in the card game of "Tagwar" in the film *Bang the Drum Slowly*. In it, baseball players hustle unsuspecting fans by engaging them in a card game that has no rules. Any attempt to imitate the players' moves implodes on itself because they never do anything the same way twice. The "speech" of parrots provides yet another example of the difference between mere imitation and meaningful participation. Nevertheless, imitative reciprocity remains inextricably bound up with the acquisition of speech and understanding.

This brings us to the final consideration of the present chapter. Reciprocal imitative activity is given its meaning in relation to the specific tasks that the participants are seeking to accomplish in a given context. It is extremely important to see how crucial the pragmatic dimension was to the Kaufmans' program with Raun. It was by tying their games and speech-acts to their son's everyday needs that they were able to mesh the gears of his private world with those of their own, public world. Specifically, the episodes in which they tried to get Raun to use their simplified vocabulary in place of crying to express his wants and needs clearly illustrate this. Much like any foreigner who is stranded in a remote place and must use what little of the local language he or she knows, Raun was forced into using the few words his parents were teaching him. As he found that these sounds actually got for him the things he wanted, he began to use them more and more.

It appears that the actual turning point for Raun came in connection with the word for water, "wa." One cannot help but be reminded of Helen Keller's account of her own breakthrough into speech while standing at the water pump, water pouring over her hand, as her teacher repeatedly spelled the word "water" into her other hand. She even uttered "Wawa," presumably harkening back to the word she had learned prior to her deafness at age fifteen months. In any case, what is important for our purposes here is that in both of these cases the learner was being confronted by a teacher within the context of a real-life situation. In addition, the respective contexts involved a good deal of emotional pressure to get a specific task accomplished.

In this way we can see that there are two interrelated dimensions involved in the acquisition of language, the first being that of imitative, even playful reciprocal activity and the second being that of pragmatic, even emotionally pressured urgency to accomplish a specific task. The Kaufmans' work with Raun clearly exemplifies both.

5

Psychology, Language, and Knowledge

Throughout the previous chapters the focus has been on specific cases of chimps and individual children who seem to hover around the threshold of language in fascinating ways. Each of these cases raises the central concern of this book, namely, the mystery of language acquisition. It is now time to pay some attention to the experiments and findings of those scientists working to provide an empirical basis for understanding the mystery that is language. Generally, this field of study is labeled "psycholinguistics," since it explores the interface between cognitive psychology and linguistics. My primary source for the consideration of the work being done in this field is a recent collection of studies edited by Paul Bloom, entitled *Language Acquisition.*

Due to the empirical nature of studies in this discipline, certain experimental procedures and techniques are employed in order to control variables and ensure objectivity. The positive benefits of such methodology are familiar and obvious. Frequently overlooked, however, are the philosophical presuppositions built into all attempts to understand a complex and multidimensional phenomenon exclusively in terms of the experimental method. Any such attempt may well systematically eliminate various aspects of the reality in question by its very nature. In short, the processes involved in language acquisition during an artificially contrived experiment are not necessarily the same as those at work in a natural setting.

Specifically, in nearly every case various groups of children are assembled in unfamiliar rooms and placed in front of television screens or special devices under "laboratory conditions" by unfamiliar people. Moreover, the children are generally asked to respond to specific stimuli or to perform certain unrelated tasks in a context that has no real connection with their normal, everyday world and experience. Finally, their performance is usually measured and quantified in terms of statistical averages. To be sure, it is possible to gather a great deal of interesting data in this fashion, but it is not clear just what such data can tell us about the actual learning of speech itself.

In this chapter, therefore, I shall seek to raise and explore the theoretic implications of the methodology used by those working in the field of psycholinguistics. I am especially concerned with those dimensions of language acquisition that are neglected by this method, as revealed by the character of the vocabulary employed and by the nature of the experimental studies themselves. Concretely, I have in mind the somatic, pragmatic, and social interaction dimensions that have already been seen to initiate and shape a child's enculturation into the human speaking community. Any approach to the understanding of language acquisition that ignores these factors will necessarily be extremely one-sided and one-dimensional.

Key Features Overlooked

A number of important features of the process of acquiring language are missing from most psycholinguistic studies. For one thing, there is generally little discussion of the so-called prelinguistic phase of the early months of a child's life, during which time there is a great deal of interactive verbal exchange between an infant and its main counter part in the speaking community. In addition to various noisemaking activities and games, such as pattycake, there usually are songs and specific verbal rituals that take place. It is this period of verbal "free play" that serves as the matrix out of which arise all the features of language that the researchers in this field are concerned with. Any attempt to come to an understanding of how speech is acquired can hardly afford to neglect this highly formative period.

To be more specific, it is certainly during this phase of children's lives that the imitative character of their mode of interaction with speakers takes shape. Moreover, it should be very clear that this imitative mode is absolutely crucial to the entire enterprise of acquiring language. Children instinctively seek to imitate the sounds by which they are surrounded, and from these they move to an increasingly complex level of interaction involving actual participation in the speaking community. These early imitative activities surely carry all the earmarks of "proto-conversations" and as such bear a good deal of scrutiny.

Another related phenomenon that is generally overlooked by researchers in this field is the fact that small children generally learn how to distinguish and even employ the various intonations characteristic of different speech-acts, such as declarative, imperative, and interrogative, well before they acquire any real vocabulary or grammatical sense. Every parent has overheard his or her child intently engaged in "conversations," perhaps on a play telephone, in which the child gives orders, makes statements, asks questions, and even tells jokes (or at least laughs at them) without the use of actual words. Here again we see the roots of speech being formed by means of minimal participation based on the process of imitation. Such roots cannot go unexamined if we wish to understand how children learn to speak.

This mention of the cruciality of interactive participation points up yet another frequent omission on the part of those working in psycholinguistics, one that has even more serious consequences. Although some effort is made to treat gestures as an important feature of language acquisition, generally only those that can be construed as symbolic are taken into consideration. This leaves entirely unexplored those that are inextricably bound up with general body language. To investigate language, and especially its initial acquisition, in such a way as to ignore its somatic grounding is to distort one's understanding from the outset. Such features as facial expression and posture are integrally related to the actual practice of speaking at the deepest possible level and must be considered as pivotal in the acquisition of language.

This oversight is particularly evident whenever researchers discuss the phenomenon of pointing. Almost without exception, they either take pointing as simply another symbolic gesture or they assume that it is somehow fundamental to the first stages of language because it establishes the basic connection between referential terms and their referents, between words and the world. Few, if any, even raise the question of how a child ever learns to read and engage in pointing in the first place. It is clear, to be sure, that we cannot teach a child how to do these things by pointing to pointing itself, since this presupposes that they already know what pointing means. In fact, pointing functions as an excellent metonymy for language in general, for neither can be explained in terms of themselves, yet each emerges on the linguistic scene as if devoid of antecedents. Here again the somatic axis of language stands in need of much greater attention than it has received.

The work of Maurice Merleau-Ponty, which has been presented in other chapters in this book, provides an excellent jumping-off point for an investigation of the highly significant act of pointing. His efforts to locate human embodiment as the axis of cognition and speech, in his monumental *Phenomenology of Perception*, establish a crucial connection between physical activity and linguistic interaction in the world. The linchpin of this connection is the merging of gesture and pointing on the one hand with language and knowledge on the other. Language is more than "talking heads."

One other omission strikes me as extremely important to this entire endeavor. As near as I am able to tell, there is little, if any, attention paid to the notion of metaphorical speech and its possible role in language acquisition. The reason for this is not difficult to guess; almost all of those working in this field begin by assuming that metaphoric or "figurative" expression will be understood by children and by those of us studying it only after they or we have come to understand referential or "literal" expression. This in spite of the fact that we generally explain literal speech as comprising "dead metaphors" and pride ourselves on having risen above "mythic" language by means of "scientific" language, both of which clearly entail that the metaphoric mode is logically prior to the so-called literal mode of speech.

Perhaps the most helpful way to explain the initial efforts we and children make to connect up our sounds with the world around us is in terms of metaphor. When any set of objects is classified by being given a "name," what we are doing essentially is proposing some sort of similarity between a known member of the class and the others. We are in effect saying that these aspects or objects are like or are somehow related to the known one, say, a dog or a chair. In fact, we are saying those *are* this in this particular respect. We thereby establish a relationship by means of asserting an identity; in short, we affirm a relationship through the use of metaphor. Language simply cannot begin with names of isolated particulars, and thus all class terms are initially metaphoric.

An initial and extremely insightful effort at exploring the connections between the somatic dimension of human existence and the metaphoric dimension of linguistic activity can be found in the book *Metaphors We Live By* by George Lakoff and Mark Johnson. The chapter entitled "Orientational Metaphors" is especially informative with respect to the way in which and the degree to which human language is woven in and around our interaction with the spatial environment. Not only is our ability to perceive and negotiate the world around us largely a function of how we construe it spatially, but much of the value system by means of which we order our lives is projected in and through spatial metaphors. Feeling "up" or "down," evaluating events as "upward" or "downward" trends, and classifying people as "insiders" or "outsiders" (us and them) are expressions that have a clear basis in such physical characteristics as posture, size, and proximity. Here is how the authors put the matter:

> Such metaphorical orientations are not arbitrary. They have a basis in our physical and cultural experience. Though the polar oppositions up-down, in-out, etc., are physical in nature, the orientational metaphors based on them can vary from culture to culture . . . or consider the nonspatial orientation active-passive. For us active is up and passive is down in most matters. But there are cultures where passivity is valued more than activity. (pp. 14, 24)

Vocabulary and Presuppositions

Two areas of theoretic concern raise profound questions for the very way in which psycholinguists set out to study language acquisition in the first place. The first set of questions pertains to the specific vocabulary employed when these thinkers discuss how a child learns to use language. The second has to do with the nature of the experiments that are used in seeking to isolate various aspects of this highly complex yet extremely natural phenomenon. Both of these sorts of questions focus deep issues about the nature of language and knowledge that most researchers in this field fail to address at all.

The vocabulary used to describe the speech behavior of children generally is, almost without exception, very "mentalistic" in character. As such it buys into a specific paradigm concerning the nature of cognitivity, one that clearly begs the very question being explored. More specifically, such researchers almost invariably speak of the child who is learning language as if he or she were an adult who is capable of employing the hypothetico-deductive method of reasoning. Let me offer a number of examples of the sort of thing I mean and then move to indicating precisely what is pernicious about this way of speaking. It is important to bear in mind that the following examples are the rule rather than the exception.

Paul Bloom, in his introduction to *Language Acquisition,* introduces the terms "hypothesis," "mechanisms," and "infer" when describing the acquisition process. He says:

> A constraint theorist might argue that regardless of how some mothers might aid children in the process of word learning, children are still faced with a logical infinity of candidate hypotheses—and psychologists have to develop a theory of the sorts of mental mechanisms that allow children to infer the correct hypothesis from the linguistic and non-linguistic context that they are exposed to. (p. 17)

Unfortunately, no reason is given as to why such "mental mechanisms" are necessary or even appropriate to an explanation of the learning process. In her discussion in the same volume, Ellen Markman also employs the term "hypotheses," but in addition she introduces the terms "concepts," "encodes," "rejects," and "evidence" (p. 155).

Also in this book, Melissa Bowerman introduces her discussion of cognitive predispositions with an account of the impact of the theories of cognitive psychologists on linguistic acquisition. In so doing, she makes the following statements: "As children begin to want to communicate, they search for linguistic forms . . . that will allow them to encode their ideas" (p. 329). Here we see the mentalistic assumption exerting itself in such terms as "ideas," "search," and "encode." Adult processes are once more projected onto the behavior of very young children without any attempt to explain or support why this is assumed to be appropriate. This way of speaking sets up a picture of the child carrying on a reasoning process that requires the use of inductive inference *prior to* having become a true member of the speaking community. This way of proceeding skews the entire investigation before it gets off the ground.

One of the chief difficulties with basing the entire enterprise of coming to an understanding of language acquisition in and on the sort of terminology highlighted in the above quotations is that it begs important questions as to the nature of human communication. The mentalistic quality of this vocabulary entails a commitment to the "picture theory of meaning" derived from the philosophy of logical empiricism as developed by Bertrand Russell and the young Ludwig Wittgenstein. To conceive of meaning as a function of isolated units that serve to connect individual words with various objects and qualities in the world, and are contained within the child's mind, simply fails to do justice to the multifarious character of human speech. Such a "luggage-tag" theory of meaning necessitates a view of both language and reality best described by Russell as "Logical Atomism," a view now completely discredited by the insights of the later Wittgenstein.

On the one hand, as Gestalt psychologists have made exceedingly clear, the world is experienced and understood, even by children, not as divisible into independent units but as meaningful wholes that only later can be analyzed into what we call "parts." On the other hand, neither can linguistic meaning be accounted for by means of a "building block" theory that ignores the social and pragmatic basis of communication. Neither adults nor children go around with individual meanings in their heads that they seek to encode into speech so as to "picture" the world around them. Speech is understood holistically, and meaning is a function of use.

Let me sketch out some helpful themes from the work of the later Wittgenstein by way of suggesting a more fruitful approach to the understanding of linguistic meaning. One of his insights concerns the way in which the different uses of a term or an expression are related, not by sharing a common essential meaning but by a series of criss-crossing and overlapping similarities that Wittgenstein called "family resemblances." As the members of a family often look alike without sharing any one common characteristic, so the different uses of a term can be related without having a common "meaning." Here is how Wittgenstein put it:

> Consider for example the proceedings that we call "games." I mean board-games, ball-games, Olympic games, and so on. What is common

to them all? Don't say: "There must be something common, or they would not be called 'games'"—but *look and see* whether there is anything common to all. For if you look at them you will not see something that is common to *all*, but similarities, relationships, and a whole series of them at that. (*Philosophical Investigations*, #66)

This use of the family resemblance metaphor by Wittgenstein is but one of a whole myriad of metaphors employed by him in order to highlight the organic character of language in contrast to the static atomism of the picture theory of meaning. I once collected a list of expressions that employ the term "hand" in order to demonstrate this notion of family resemblance in linguistic meaning. The list included such expressions as "secondhand," "underhand," "hand-in-hand," "hand-to-mouth," "handy," "handsome," "offhand," "hands-down," and "hand over-fist." It should be clear that these terms do not share in a common, definitive meaning. Rather, each is introduced by means of a fresh, metaphoric connection that is not merely an extension of a former meaning but an organic reproduction that takes on a life of its own.

Another of Wittgenstein's metaphors that sheds light here is that of the contrast between an ancient city and a modern one. He likens everyday language to the older city that lies at the center of the metropolis. The streets run in odd yet practical patterns, the architecture is diverse, and various features seem quaint and cumbersome. Nevertheless it is here that people initially lived and worked, even as they built the surrounding suburbs with their well-planned facilities and evenly laid-out streets. It is the diversity and complexity of the "old city" at the center of ordinary speech that functions as the ground of meaning. All trips to the clarity and order of the "suburbs" of scientific method and the like must begin and return here (*Philosophical Investigations*, #18).

The difficulty that arises here is that the thinkers who create and work in the suburbs of language come to think of them as their natural home, or at least as the ideal dwelling place. This seems to be the problem with those working in the field of psycholinguistics. They seek to project the highly specialized way of thinking onto children engaged in language acquisition, thus distorting our understanding from the very outset. Since even adult thought and speech do not conform to such mechanistic and strict patterns, it is hardly to be expected that those of children would do so.

One final difficulty with this "linguist mentalism" merits mention. The entire project of seeking to explain the cognitive processes involved in a child's acquisition of its first language in terms of highly articulated rational procedures is part and parcel of the deeper and more widespread error of attempting to explain all forms of understanding on the basis of external processes and mechanisms. One does not have to embrace behaviorism in order to object to the assumption that thinking and speaking are separable operations. In fact, as Wittgenstein and Gilbert Ryle have established, it really is not helpful to construe thinking as a process, as a kind of inner speech, at all. To invent all sorts of "mechanisms" at work in the child's mind, called "hypotheses," "inferences," and "concepts," is no more enlightening than inventing "egos," "ids," and "super-egos" has proven to be. Perhaps it would be more helpful to speak of skills rather than mechanisms. I shall return to this suggestion shortly.

A specific problem that arises from the way thinkers in psycholinguistics talk about the child's acquisition of language is that it actually explains nothing at all. The terms introduced to account for the learning of language are really just shorthand descriptions of the behavior that they are supposed to explain. To say that a child "infers" or "deduces" the meaning of an utterance is simply another way of saying that she or he now uses and responds to the utterance appropriately. But we already know this; what we are after is an explanation, not a reiteration of this fact. The same can be said for Noam Chomsky's famous "Language Acquisition Device," or LAD. How does it help us to be told that children acquire language by virtue of their innate ability to acquire language? This is not an explanation but, rather, another name for the phenomenon under examination, just as it is of no help to be told that sleeping pills induce sleep because of their "soporific power."

All in all, then, the essentially consistent vocabulary used by writers in this field reveals a completely unaddressed set of assumptions concerning the nature and function of both thought and speech, a set of assumptions that lead to a distorted interpretation of the acquisition of one's natural language. At least one way to focus the erroneous character of the approach that underlies much of the work going on in psycholinguistics is to point out that it is far more appropriate to an account of how humans learn a second or third language than it is to how they acquire their mother tongue. Hypotheses, meanings, inferences, and the like would be relevant to an account of how a person would proceed if set down in the midst of a community where he or she was entirely unfamiliar with the language. From personal experience many of us know that we would reason from our experience with our native tongue through our encounter with the new environment to knowledge of the unknown language. That is, we would reason our way from square one to square two. But to talk this way about how we got from square zero to square one in the first place is unhelpful at best and debilitating at worst.

In the end the mistake involved in all this is a failure to acknowledge the fact that to a very large extent, if not entirely, our ability to engage in various forms of inductive and deductive reasoning of the type entailed by the vocabulary used in psycholinguistic explorations of language acquisition is achieved along with, if not after and on the basis of, our ability to participate in language. In a word, we learn to reason with and by speech. Thus it is quite misleading, to say the least, to analyze our acquisition of the latter in terms of the former. To be sure, Piaget made a good case for the claim that children exhibit the ability to reason prior to speech, but his case is flawed by the fact that he defined speech so narrowly that he failed to treat the first eighteen months at all, to say nothing of ignoring the "protolinguistic" period altogether.

Moreover, as Piaget saw, the sort of reasoning that prelinguistic children display is primarily somatic in character, embodied in their interaction with the physical environment, and this is precisely the area of a child's cognitive activity that serves as the matrix for his or her conscious reasoning powers and symbolic discourse. Furthermore, this is precisely the area that is left almost completely unexplored in much of the work being done by those working in psycholinguistics. Far too frequently the implication is that a child's mind is nothing but a "ghost in a machine," as Ryle so aptly put it. One would have thought that by now this ghost, along with the dualistic philosophy that spawned it, would have been exorcised.

Experiments and Presuppositions

The second area of theoretic concern that current psycholinguistic research language acquisition focuses on has to do with the question of methodology. It is the nature of the experimental approach to this phenomenon that raises serious issues about what knowledge is and how it is achieved. Although there is little question about the general value of the experimental method in general, it is not at all clear that the specific sort of experiments used by those working in this field are appropriate to the nature of the task.

The main bother is that nearly all the experiments set up to study various aspects and specific features of the child's acquisition of language are extremely artificial and quite isolated from the dynamics of normal speech contexts and learning processes. The chief difficulty lies with the fact that these experiments are conducted as if language were carried on in a mentalistic vacuum by solitary speakers completely disengaged from each other and from the tasks of real, everyday life. In a sense this problem may well be the flip side of that discussed in the previous section. At bottom it is the overriding tendency of such researchers to treat linguistic cognitivity as a process of matching the images in a child's mind with objects and qualities in the physical world that undermines their efforts from the outset.

In the majority of cases the children being studied in the various experiments are placed in situations that are contrived rather than natural. That is to say, they are set in front of mechanical or electronic devices and asked to "observe" what takes place before them and respond to different questions. In parallel cases the children are asked to observe other people, usually adults, and answer questions about what they are doing. The following is a typical example from Bloom's book:

> Consider the learning of certain motion verbs, such as *push* or *move*. In a satisfying proportion of the times that caretakers say something like "George pushes the truck," George can be observed pushing the truck. But . . . every time he pushes the truck, the truck will move. So a verb used by the caretaker to describe this event may represent one of these ideas ("push") or the other ("move"). (p. 183)

Even when the author is arguing that a child cannot learn the differences involved in such cases from observation alone, as Lila Gleitman is doing here, this conclusion itself is based on yet other experiments wherein children respond to questions about what they have passively observed going on in front of them.

The problem is that such artificial situations in which children are confronted with various "talking heads" may not have much to do with the way language is actually acquired in real-life situations. In other words, the methodological "net" being used to capture what is going on in learning to speak may systematically fail to catch the very item being sought because the net is in fact the wrong size.

What is missing from these experiments, and it may be the case that this is endemic to experiments per se, is the natural, pragmatic context within which children actually do acquire language. From the minute they arrive on the scene, tiny infants are involved with the world around them, not simply as observers but as participants. Not only are they continuously addressed as if they understand what is being said to them, but they are related to and moved around in ways that incorporate them into the world. Things are happening around them and with them; things are getting done along with and by means of what is being said by members of the speaking community, of which they are fast becoming an integral part. In short, even very young children are players, not mere observers, in the various language games comprised by the world around them.

As they continue to grow, they take on an increasingly active role in these pragmatic contexts, making requests, following directions, eating, singing, going places, and so on. In all this they absorb rather than infer the "meaning" of the utterances in which they are immersed by actually participating in the activities, not merely observing them. The meaning of the locutions with which they are surrounded is inextricably bound up with the activities of which they are part and parcel. Thus, to attempt to understand the acquisition process by constructing experiments that are devoid of this crucial pragmatic dimension of language wherein actual tasks get accomplished in the real world surely leaves a great deal to be desired.

The other side of this pragmatic coin is that of the somatic character of the contexts within which children learn to speak. Not only do things happen and get done around them, but things happen and get done to and by them as well. Children are, after all, embodied creatures, and their speech arises amid the interplay of their bodies with physical objects and other embodied persons. When they are little, people pick them up and move them around, and as they grow, they themselves begin to move around and move objects around. Although all this is obvious enough, the somatic dimension of the acquisition process is sorely lacking from the majority of the experiments presented and discussed in many, if not most, reports. The children generally sit still, observe, and respond to specific and isolated questions — talking heads again.

The organic and dynamic quality of speech acquisition is systematically excluded by the design of the experiments in question. Long before they are taught the "meanings" of specific terms and expressions, small children are both exposed to the linguistic activity of adults, as well as older children, and participate in the speech dimension of the give-and-take, task orientation of daily life. Not only are they given simple commands and answers ("Stop!" and "No"), but they are asked questions ("How are you today?" "What do you want?"), given requests ("Please don't do that," "Would you come over here?"), and offered explanations ("Do it like this," "This is hot"). In each of these cases the meaning of the utterance, in the sense of definitions or concepts, is completely beyond the child. Nevertheless, its functional meaning is soon grasped because of and by means of the pragmatic interaction between the speakers, the physical or social setting, and their own responses. One can learn, indeed must learn, the meaning of such expressions as "Don't walk on the rug" and "Bring me the book" long before learning any definitions of the terms comprised by them. It is only by means of the former that the latter can be learned, for apart from a pragmatic context it is not possible to grasp definitional meanings.

Yet another facet of the difficulty caused by the sort of experiments employed by these researchers is that they force one to overlook what might be termed the social aspect of language. The replies that the children being studied give to the questions put to them about what they observe are unilateral or one-dimensional. In a very real sense, these answers are given in a vacuum because they do not plug into any real, ongoing conversation. To put it differently, the children's replies are not really given to anyone in particular but, rather, are simply part of a kind of abstract recitation, somewhat like a test or word game. My point is not that we cannot learn a good deal from such experiments but that it is unclear whether they can tell us very much about the acquisition of language since they are so stilted and devoid of real-life, social interaction. There clearly are cases wherein the nature of the methodological instrument precludes the possibility of obtaining the very sort of knowledge aimed at.

Perhaps it is possible to trace the source of the difficulty inherent within this experimental approach to the unconscious assumption of those designing them that children must acquire their first language by means of essentially the same rational procedures that adults use in acquiring a second or third language. Although such an assumption would appear to be ludicrous on the face of it, the quotations set forth in the previous sections of this chapter make it altogether clear that it is constantly operative in the way these researchers go about their work. A particularly straightforward example of what I have in mind is the following statement, previously quoted, from Melissa Bowerman's essay: "As children begin to want to communicate, they search for the linguistic forms . . . that will allow them to encode their ideas" (Bloom, p. 329). Even though Bowerman disavows the point of view she is describing here, her way of putting the matter remains highly representative of the mentality of which I am speaking.

The adult character of this way of describing the child engaged in language learning is patently obvious. The very notion of a young child having ideas prior to speech and then looking around for the proper way to put them into words is questionable at best and comical at worst. Even adults rarely separate their thinking from their speech in such a manner, unless, of course, they are operating in a highly specialized context, such as a second language. There are many thinkers who maintain that ideas emerge as the result of linguistic interaction, rather than the other way around. The mystery of the relationship between thought and language is extremely complex, even at the adult level.

Perhaps the most alarming thing about the adult character of these experimenters' manner of describing the dynamics of the child's first language acquisition is its complete lack of awareness of the role played by imitation. To says things like "As children begin to want to communicate, they search for linguistic forms" is to betray a gross ignorance of how children actually do enter into speech well before they begin to search for words. Anyone who has ever paid attention to small children is aware that they actually force their way into the speaking community by attempting to imitate, no matter how poorly, the speech of those around them. The fact is, children arrive on the scene desiring to communicate and to be incorporated into the language games going on around them. By means of imitation they slowly, or not so slowly, come to participate in human discourse long before they search for linguistic forms. To separate this prelinguistic activity from the process of language acquisition by focusing exclusively on the learning of words and grammar is to fail to see the forest for the trees.

Some Constructive Suggestions

As should be more than clear by now, my fundamental problem with the psycholinguistic approach is its theoretical naiveté concerning the implications of its methodology with respect to the concepts of language and knowledge. The basic difficulty is that cognitivity is defined strictly in terms of mental awareness and processes rather than as a function of the whole person and somatic skills in a pragmatic, social context. Both cognitivity and linguistic meaning need to be reconceived so as to be understood as rooted in embodied, interactive processes out of which arise mental states and inferential abilities.

The trouble is that when psycholinguistic researchers attempt to investigate the mystery of language further, they continue to do so on the basis of the dysfunction between two traditional ways of setting the problem up, namely, innate categories and associative exposure. This simply perpetuates the problem. In Bloom's book Eve Clark and Kathie Carpenter suggest a pattern of interplay between these two disjuncts that allows the latter, experiential input to reveal the former, structural patterns. Thus the innate categories are said to "emerge" in and through experiential interaction.

> Emergent categories reflect the conceptual similarities perceived by children among paradigms or structures, even where these similarities are obscured by the conventional forms of the language. Emergent categories offer evidence for the conceptual representations that underlie linguistic categories and that have linguistic consequences. (p. 272)

Although this is a helpful way to put the matter, it still offers no explanation of the nature of the innate structures or of the dynamics whereby they can be said to "emerge." The difficulty continues to be the demand that somehow the acquisition process must be explained in terms of explicable rules or categories by means of which the child assimilates and organizes its experiential input. The assumption is that the principles of cognitivity must, in the final analysis, be articulatable. It is generally said that the only alternative to this assumption is to admit that such structural rules are inaccessible and call it quits.

Fortunately, D. E. Rumelhart and J. L. McClelland, also in Bloom's book, suggest that there might be another way to conceive of the relationship between structural rules and linguistic exposure.

> We propose an alternative to explicit inaccessible rules. We suggest that lawful behavior and judgments may be produced by a mechanism in which there is no explicit representation of the rule. Instead, we suggest that the mechanisms that process language and make judgments of grammaticality are constructed in such a way that their performance is characterizable by rules, but that the rules themselves are not written in explicit form anywhere in the mechanism. (p. 424)

Later in the book, Annette Karmiloff-Smith develops a similar line of thought in seeking to overcome what she calls the nativist versus the constructivist impasse. She proposes a "representational redescription" hypothesis in which the human mind consciously re-represents recursively its own internal representations, which are produced by lower-level innate structures. In this process

> the lower levels are left intact; copies of these are redescribed. Redescription involves a loss, at the higher level, of information that continues to be represented at the lower level. Our multiple levels of representation are not . . . simple duplicates of lower levels; rather, they involve increasing explication and accessibility at the cost of detail of information. (p. 569)

The upshot of the foregoing suggestions is the demand for a more comprehensive redefinition of cognitive activity in general. The only way to avoid the stalemates resulting from the standard "rationalist versus empiricist" debate is to approach the question of knowledge from a more holistic and dynamic perspective, one that does not begin by separating the mind from the body. The focus of the attempt to understand language acquisition needs to be shifted from an analysis of exclusively mentalistic structures and processes to an exploration of the interactive character of a child's embodied and social behavior. The following sketch is offered as a down payment toward such an exploration.

To begin with, it is helpful to think of human experience as comprising two dimensions, the awareness dimension and the activity dimension. The former has as its poles subsidiary and focal awareness. In every situation we are aware of some things focally and of others subsidiarily. The reader is now, or was until now, only subsidiarily aware that his or her feet are in shoes or that I am using written symbols to communicate ideas. Now the reader has been made focally aware of these facts. We always attend from some aspects of our environment to others, even though what is focal in one context may become subsidiary in another and vice versa.

The poles of the activity dimension of human experience are conceptual activity and bodily activity. Although there may be no hard and fast division between these, generally we can distinguish them from each other. Doing math problems in one's head and running the hundred-meter dash are significantly different activities. Moreover, from birth onward we tend to incorporate ever-increasing degrees of conceptual activity, even though our thought life continues to be dependent on our physical life in a fundamental fashion.

Now when these two dimensions of human experience intersect, yet a third, more complex dimension emerges, namely, that of cognitivity. The interaction between focal awareness and conceptual activity gives rise to one pole of this cognitivity dimension, while that between subsidiary awareness and bodily activity gives rise to the other. The former pole may be designated "explicit knowing," and the latter "tacit knowing." Explicit knowing involves the isolation of particulars, precise definitions, objective descriptions, and the articulation of rationales. Tacit knowing, on the other hand, includes a range of experience that is usually ignored or denied cognitive status because it is not articulatable within the rubrics of explicit knowing. The main reason that tacit knowing is not explicable is that it is rooted in the body and is expressed in skills rather than in concepts.

Tacit knowing is a function of the reciprocal interplay between the full range of bodily activity amid the vast amount of subsidiary exposure provided by the environment. This is what Michael Polanyi, in his extremely profound book *Personal Knowledge*, calls the process of "indwelling," the dynamic whereby we immerse our embodied selves in the almost infinite number of features of our surroundings. The meaning Gestalts formed by means of this dynamic of indwelling are not the result of inferential processes involving hypotheses and deductive selection. They are, rather, the result of what Polanyi terms "integrative acts" effected by our motor and sensory abilities, which in turn provide the basis for the development of both bodily and eventually conceptual skills.

This way of construing cognitivity makes it evident that tacit knowing provides the axis around which explicit knowing revolves, for the former is logically prior to the latter. In all knowing our point of entry is through our embodied indwelling of the subsidiary factors to which we are exposed; we seek to grasp objects, walk, and talk by directing our embodied intentionality toward the world, both physical and social. As such, all explicit knowing is anchored in tacit skills that are neither produced by nor fully articulatable in terms of the categories and processes of explicit knowing.

My suggestion is that when the phenomenon of language acquisition is understood according to the above model of cognitive activity, the dilemmas plaguing many if not most psycholinguistic approaches can be overcome. Moreover, the insights of those researchers cited at the outset of this section can also be seen in their best light. However, it is first necessary to set aside the assumption that all human knowledge can and must be understood by means of an intellectualist model. As Polanyi says, "We always know more than we can tell."

From this perspective it seems clear that children, beginning as newborn infants, are immersed in the medium of language in much the same way they come to exist in and breathe oxygen. They come to indwell social reality through their "enlanguagement" even as they come to indwell physical reality through their embodiment. At first this immersion produces only subsidiary awareness, although it would be a mistake to think of this level of experience as passive in character. As the world "comes at" the child, both physically and verbally, so the child comes into the world seeking meaning and making judgments. As the child interacts with the diffuse, undifferentiated sea of sounds and accompanying activity, specific integrative acts occur that in turn provide the behavioral gestalts for the formation of further meaning-closures. From this tacit axis the child moves toward explicit articulation in speech, at first in terms of responses, requests, names, and questions, and later in terms of concepts, rules, and reasonings.

The crucial factor here is the notion of tacit knowing being rooted in subsidiary awareness and bodily activity, so that its cognitive import is seen as being appropriately and exclusively expressed in terms of skills rather than mental processes. The empiricist, behaviorist, or associativist account of language acquisition emphasizes mere exposure and physical response, failing to understand either the subsidiary character of the child's linguistic awareness or the embodied intentionality of the wider speaking community. The rationalist, structuralist, or nativist account emphasizes the equipment or capacities which the child initially brings to linguistic reality, but neglects both the crucial role of bodily activity as the matrix of linguistic meaning and the task-centered orientation of the speaking community. The model advocated here synthesizes these two approaches by positing tacit knowing as the ground of language acquisition, rather than explicit intellectual procedures.

The crux of the proposal being made here can be summarized in terms of the notion of "bootstrapping" (Steven Pinker's term in *The Language Instinct*). Both nativists and constructionists employ this concept in terms of syntax or semantics, respectively, to explain how a child moves from square zero to square one, two, and so on linguistically. What gets overlooked, however, is the simple point that as a matter of fact it is always impossible for one to lift oneself by the bootstraps. Once the assumption has been made that all cognitive activity must be based on and expressed in articulatable, explicit structures and processes, it is not possible to explain how children acquire language. You just can't get here from there! The distance from square zero to square one, from being prelinguistic to speaking, cannot be covered by means of the same principles as that from square one to subsequent squares, since the latter case is quantitative while the former is qualitative. Only by tracing language acquisition to its tacit, behavioral roots can one understand how the skill of speech is acquired.

6

Forked Tongues, Otherness, and Understanding

There is an old and politically incorrect joke that focuses the themes of this chapter extremely well. It seems that the Lone Ranger and Tonto were surrounded by thousands of Indians and the Masked Man turned to Tonto and asked, "What are we going to do?" Whereupon Tonto replied, "What do you mean *we*, white man?" The intersection of questions of linguistic meaning and political realities in this brief scenario points up yet another dimension of the difficulties surrounding any attempt to get a fix on the threshold of language. On the following pages I shall explore this dimension at various levels and offer some suggestions as to how the cognitive difficulties involved might be resolved. As a map and initial guide for these explorations, I shall use David Murray's fascinating book *Forked Tongues: Speech, Writing, and Representation in North American Indian Texts*. My aim is to establish that the threshold of language is not as problematic as the theorists trying to explain it would have us believe.

Three Levels of Analysis

Murray's book operates on at least three levels simultaneously. His primary focus is on the mediating role of the interpreter or translator in the communication and transmission of North American Indian speech. On the first page of his introduction, Murray states that one of his main aims is "to demonstrate the complex and various ways in which the process of translation, cultural as well as linguistic, is obscured or effaced in a wide variety of texts which claim to be representing or describing Indians." In fulfilling this purpose, Murray works his way through quite a number of translations and representations of specific Indian utterances, speeches, and writings, as well as a good many "theories" about Indian languages offered by various interpreters and translators in the eighteenth and nineteenth centuries.

This level of Murray's study is rich in research data and original insights. On the one hand, he provides a great deal of textual material containing the actual speeches and writings of a number of rather celebrated Indian characters, most of whom served as informants and go-betweens for early New England missionaries and educators. On the other hand, he also documents a wide selection of communications from various white interpreters of Indian languages and culture, some of whom were quite influential in their day, such as the son of Jonathan Edwards. In case after case Murray traces the interesting intricacies and reciprocal dynamics of the exchanges among these early participants in the cultural interface between Indian and white societies. There is a great deal of material here for the student of cultural and linguistic anthropology.

At a different level, Murray is also engaged in revealing and wrestling with the political dimension of these early linguistic and cultural interchanges. He wants to clarify the "ideological assumptions" that underlie the particular manner in which the linguistic behavior of Indians was represented or described. Here is where the significance of Murray's use of the term "forked tongues" comes to light. For, like Tonto and other well-known Hollywood Indians, Murray maintains that "white men speak with forked-tongue," that when white interpreters spoke of Indian speech and behavior they said two opposing things at the same time. In the case of Murray's subjects, however, the claim is that for the most part the duplicity was unconscious, for the interpreters actually thought they were simply describing Indian linguistic behavior. Nevertheless, in so doing they actually helped create inscrutable "others."

The fact remains, however, according to Murray, that the hidden cultural and political agenda underlying the entire white perspective on and approach to Indians necessarily involved assumptions about (1) their "savage" and retarded character in relation to white peoples and cultures and (2) the importance of maintaining this cultural inferiority so as to justify and facilitate America's "Manifest Destiny." It is here that "postmodernist" tone enters into Murray's approach, since

it enables, indeed demands, that we see the "double meaning" possibilities inherent within the white, ostensibly "objective" representation of Indians.

The depth and subtlety of Murray's analysis of the hidden political
agenda are shown by his suggestion that even when the picture of the
savage Indian became that of the "Noble Savage," the basic intent remained the same. Thus the speeches of Chief Seattle, Chief Joseph,
Black Elk, and others, while aimed at castigating white genocide of the
Indian race and environmental rape, reinforced the inevitability of
such atrocities. "The dramatic career of the noble Indian who dies out
practically and politically, but survives in his words as a monument,
an occasion for suitably comfortable melancholy reflections" (p. 37)
places the plight and fate of the Indian race on a higher moral plane
than the white race, thereby allowing whites to feel properly guilty and
ennobled while simultaneously continuing with "winning the West."

Murray does indicate that the two-way mediating position into
which such Indians were put frequently allowed them the opportunity to speak with forked tongues as well. For not only were they living with one foot in each of two quite distinct cultures and languages,
but often they were able to use this double-edged position to assert
their own Indian character and values. Occasionally this meant that
they could actually manipulate white people by turning the teachings
of their Christianized culture back toward them, vis-à-vis their culpa-
bility in supplying the whiskey that resulted in Indian drunkenness.
Murray focuses this duplicity within alienation in his discussion of
the reintroduction of the Potlatch ceremony in Kwakiutl society by
Chief Jimmy Sewid in order to raise funds for a local hospital.

> Like Geronimo selling his photographs, Black Elk performing in Wild
> West shows, or modern Indians catering for tourists, Sewid's response
> to white culture is an ambiguous one, walking the line between be-
> ing taken over and taking over, and the autobiographies discussed
> have reflected this, often not so much in the substance of the narra-
> tives as in their bicultural hybrid form, where the different registers
> of language sometimes combine and sometimes struggle for domi-
> nance. (p. 77)

The third and broadest level at which Murray's study operates pertains to the methodological and theoretical issues involved in any

attempt to understand and represent a culture markedly different from one's own. The traditional philosophical way of posing these issues is in terms of the contrast between objectivity and subjectivity. On the one side lurks the danger of allowing one's own theoretical and cultural biases to contaminate the objective, factual presentation of the reality in question. On the other side stands the objection that since one can never fully eliminate such biases, the very possibility of an objective presentation of the facts is essentially meaningless. There are even those who carry this latter position to the extreme of claiming that reality, as such, is not only in principle unknowable but is itself a meaningless notion. This basic dilemma gives rise to the problem of "otherness" within ethnographic efforts to obtain knowledge across cultures.

Within the parameters of contemporary American philosophy this debate takes the form of pitting the "critical realists" against the thoroughgoing "pragmatists." The former acknowledge the difficulties involved in the concept of objective knowledge but insist that it still makes sense to strive for an ever more reliable or accurate description of "how things are." The latter argue that what such concessions on the part of realists boil down to is the admission that knowledge is, after all, in the words of Richard Rorty, "simply a matter of what your colleagues will allow you to get away with saying." Both of these approaches to the problems involved are "postmodern" in the sense that any scientific enterprise is understood as necessarily guided by some sort of theoretical framework. In short, all "facts" are acknowledged to be "theory laden." Nevertheless, the critical realist continues to affirm the possibility of knowledge, while the pragmatist appears to be ultimately committed to relativism at best and skepticism at worst.

Within the parameters of European philosophy, these issues are taken up and developed in quite a different manner. It is within the conversation initiated by such postmodern literary and cultural critics as Michel Foucault and Jacques Derrida that Murray places his study. Here the question is expressed not in terms of objectivity and subjectivity but in terms of the denial of any privileged or established interpretative posture with respect to any utterance or written test. In fact, as has already been suggested, the claim here is that all readings of any language or text arise out of certain cultural and political assumptions and agendas that, although largely unspoken, tend to determine any interpretation of the language in question. It is these underlying interpretive factors that Murray seeks to uncover in his account of the forked-tongue phenomenon within white people's translation and representation of Indian speech and writing.

Although the issues are often joined by means of different terminologies, the crucial problem remains essentially the same. The question is, how does the unavoidable presence of theoretical presuppositions affect the possibility of obtaining knowledge? If we are too confident and naive about our putative objective accounts and understandings, we shall invariably read our own presuppositions and agendas into the reality we seek to know. If, on the other hand, we can have no confidence in our ability to know and describe any aspect of the world around us, apart from our own presuppositions and biases, we are no better off, since now we are unable to affirm any real knowledge at all. Murray is committed to discovering a mediational posture between these two extremes by focusing on dialogical interaction.

Murray becomes quite explicit in his chapter on Indian autobiography as a literary genre in which the dialogical character of this mediational role is at the forefront. Rather than seeing such accounts of Indian lives as contaminated by being presented in a form that is at odds with the patterns of oral cultures, Murray views them as the key to a dialogical understanding of anthropological knowledge: "This entails seeing them not as a corrupted and inferior form, but as a new form which reflects precisely the cultural limitations and contradictions inherent in a situation where oral and literate cultures meet" (p. 68). He also stresses the friendship ties that necessarily emerge within the human dynamics of intercultural exchange. By focusing on such dialogical factors, Murray hopes to be able to overcome the problem of "otherness."

> If one impulse of anthropology is to demonstrate the self-sufficient differentness and viability of other ways of being and experiencing the world, a complementary one is, of course, to insist on the shared human characteristics which allow us to understand and respond to members of other cultures as full human beings; one regular feature of these anthropological autobiographies is the stress in prefaces and introductions on the personal bonds of friendship between editor and subject. (p. 74)

In a similar vein, Murray discusses the character and contribution of recent trends among Indian writers by way of emphasizing the value of a more dialogical understanding of and approach to knowledge of Indian life and culture. He specifically highlights the work of, among others, N. Scott Momaday and Leslie Silko in this regard. The literary form of their novels modifies the traditional Western narrative structure so as to produce a genre more reflective of the contemporary Indian experience. "Momaday's *The Way to Rainy Mountain* (1969) uses three strands of narrative—what the author calls 'the mythical, the historical, and the immediate'—so that the retelling of the Kiowa tales of migration on to the great plains is intertwined with personal reminiscences and commentary" (p. 80). In Silko's novel *Ceremony* (1977) the main point of both the format and the story "is to advocate and exemplify the relevance and necessity of traditional concepts to modern life, rather than just accepting the terms of the modern, or drowning in nostalgia for a past that can never return as it was" (p. 80).

In his final two chapters, Murray traces out this dialogical theme found in varying degrees among the works of a number of well-known anthropologists. He considers the approaches of Franz Boaz and Claude Levi-Strauss as "salvage" and "structuralist" ethnologies, respectively. Both of these anthropological pioneers operated largely according to modernist presuppositions. In addition, Murray takes up the approaches of Frank Hamilton Cushing and Ruth Benedict, both of whom studied the Zuni Indians, but according to completely different methods. Cushing "went native" and wrote in a personal mode of his experiences, while Benedict took an objective and impersonal approach. In neither case was the notion of reciprocity crucial to their work. By way of contrast, Murray compares the perspectives of Dennis Tedlock and Carlos Castaneda. Tedlock advocates a dialogical approach, but Murray claims:

> The problem with his privileging of the native view comes if we view the role of anthropology, like any social science, as interpretive rather than descriptive, and if we acknowledge that in fact description cannot be separated and made prior to interpretation. In this case understanding rather than empathy is the ultimate goal, and this involves distance rather than closeness, difference rather than identity. Distance and difference are insisted upon not in order to preserve our

values but because the gap between cultures and the mutual estrangement (in the sense of making strange, rather than a prelude to separation and divorce) can be used as the basis of a critique, rather than a confirmation, of the values and "common sense" of both sides. (p. 147)

Carlos Castaneda, on the other hand, not only sought to blur the distinction between fictional and anthropological techniques, but "also explicitly challenges the standards of rationality which have allowed the detachment from native beliefs in the supernatural necessary to present a proper ethnographic account" (p. 153). Murray is especially interested in Castaneda's approach because it represents a dialogical fusing of the objective and the subjective, but he is also puzzled as to why Castaneda's work continues to be ignored in anthropological methodological discussions. Murray also provides a brief account of James Clifford's appropriation of Mikhail Bakhtin's insight concerning the dialogical possibilities of novelistic discourse. "Clifford describes 'an alternative textual strategy, a utopia of plural authorship' which would give collaborators the status of writers, not just 'independent enunciators'" (pp. 151–52). In this approach dialogue would be construed as taking place between texts rather than merely within texts.

Finally, Murray mentions *Yaqui Deer Songs/Maso Bwikam* (1987) by Larry Evers and Felipe Molina, which combines bilingual versions of deer songs, accompanied by cassettes, with extended discussions of their meaning and place in Yaqui culture. "The authors of this text sometimes write separately and sometimes as *we* . . . but the combination allows for an intriguing movement between viewpoints and cultures" (p. 152), with the reader-listener being the one who finally makes sense and coherence of the text. Murray concludes by referring to Steven Webster's quotation of Clifford Geertz's remarks concerning the duplicity and irony necessarily inherent within the process of anthropological research.

> To recognize the moral tension, the ethical ambiguity, implicit in the encounter of anthropologist and informant, and still be able to dissipate it through one's actions and one's attitudes, is what encounter demands of both parties if it is to discover also something very complicated and not altogether clear about the nature of sincerity and insincerity, genuineness and hypocrisy, honesty and self-deception. (p. 155)

A Self-Imposed Dilemma

By carefully analyzing the cognitivity dimension of Murray's explorations as sketched out in the foregoing section, we can see that the dilemma that Murray, along with many of the thinkers on whom he relies, finds himself in is largely one of his own making. The choice between objectivity and subjectivity, modernism and postmodernism, or universalism and relativism is itself generated by the presuppositions of traditional Western epistemology concerning the knowing subject and the known object. When these two poles of cognitive relationality are separated at the outset, it becomes impossible to avoid ending up with some form of either absolutism, mysticism, or skepticism. Even the notion of dialogue, which Murray advocates, cannot bring the subject and the object together if they are already separated by definition. All such post-facto solutions inevitably turn out to be merely cosmetic in nature.

There seem to be two main versions of the postmodern approach to the meaning and truth of linguistic activity. The first is the Derridaian literary posture, which stresses the open-textured, polysignificant character of all utterances. Since all speech is context dependent for its meaning, and since once a speaker has uttered an expression he or she no longer "owns" it, it would seem to follow that any utterances not only can be taken to mean a wide variety of things but cannot actually be said to have a meaning at all. In other words, "meanings" are constructed by those who interpret statements, with standard interpretations becoming established within a tradition. Not only can these meanings be deconstructed by altering the contexts or one's response to them, but it is useful, if not necessary, to do so in order to keep a linguistic tradition from becoming stagnant.

The second version is that of Michel Foucault, who argues that these constructed "meanings" are generally the property of those who wield political power and that they are used as tools with which to manipulate and exploit those without such power. This political dimension of the nature of linguistic activity is extremely subtle and even insidious. Indeed, it is precisely this aspect that Murray draws upon in his analysis of the ways in which Indian interpreters, including Indians themselves, constructed and maintained the traditional picture and understanding of Indian speech and culture. This dimension of speech ranges all the way from the customary exchange of greetings ("How are you?" "Fine, how are you?" "Fine"), through historical "fact" ("Columbus discovered America") and commercial advertising ("Just say 'Coke'"), to religious rituals such as confession. Murray quotes Foucault as saying:

> The confession is a ritual of discourse in which the speaking subject is also the subject of the statement; it is also a ritual that unfolds within a power relationship, for one does not confess without the presence (or virtual presence) of a partner who is not simply the interlocutor but the authority who requires the confession. (p. 51)

I have no bone to pick with either of these approaches per se. Clearly, linguistic meaning is essentially open textured and context dependent, and traditional interpretations need continually to be challenged and reshaped. Equally clearly, these linguistic traditions are frequently, if not regularly, under the control of some type of ruling class that uses them to its own advantage, and such hegemony needs continually to be questioned and reformed. What is troublesome about the way these insights get extrapolated philosophically, however, pertains to the tendency to assume an absolute separation between the speaker, the meaning, and the hearer(s) at the outset. This separation is itself predicated on the traditional Western belief that reality is fundamentally individualistic in nature. It is precisely this commitment to "atomism" that generates the very cognitive distance, together with its interpretive and political tyranny, that these theorists are so concerned with overcoming.

To put it bluntly, there is a self-stultifying, if not self-contradictory, quality about this theoretic posture. If it is assumed that all utterances are open-ended as regards their meaning, then it follows that even this utterance ("that all utterances are open-ended as regards their meaning") is itself open-ended and may not mean what it appears to mean. The sorts of confusion this kind of circular approach leads to are well illustrated in the following case. A rather well-known American philosopher gave a learned paper in which he sought to apply Derrida's insights to the field of theology, after which Derrida himself objected that he had not intended his ideas to be used in this way. The philosopher in question, quite appropriately, only smiled and asked, "So what?" The speaker's intentions, according to Derrida, have no privileged position when it comes to interpreting his or her own remarks.

The political version of the postmodern posture suffers from the same basic difficulty. If we grant that all utterances operate according to some unarticulated political agenda of manipulation or exploitation, we must go on and apply that insight to itself. What is the hidden agenda behind Foucault's claim that all discourse is an instrument of power? If we, following Murray, apply this perspective to the ways Indians have been translated and represented, do we not also have to apply it to Murray's presentation, and those of all the writers he quotes, as well? Presumably he and his colleagues are somehow different from the white interpreters of Indian life, but on what basis can we say this? Either Foucault, Murray, and even this present writer are also writing in order to "manipulate" rather than "convince" their readers, or the white interpreters may not have been. Here again, consistency entails self-stultification. What is needed is a fresh point of departure.

To being with, it must be borne in mind that an acknowledgment that any and all utterances are "packaged" within specific political agendas does not entail the falsity of the utterance in question. Just because the white interpreters of Indians had various "axes to grind," it does not follow that their representations of what the Indians said and did were erroneous. Unfortunately, however, in discussions of this type, it is often assumed that because the keepers of the tradition have complex political intentions, their utterances are untrustworthy. A vendor may say that a blanket is of "excellent quality" in order to get me to buy it, even though, in fact, the blanket *is* of excellent quality. Having mixed and unconscious motives for one's utterances does not necessarily obviate the truth of what is being asserted.

Now let us go to the heart of the matter. Near the close of his final chapter, Murray draws rather heavily on the insights of Steven Webster in order to ground his case for a dialogical approach to these issues in the philosophical position known as "critical realism." This position seeks to take a middle way between objectivism and universalism, on the one hand, and subjectivism and relativism, on the other. Critical realists claim that although personal, cultural, political, and even theoretic biases may color a given description or interpretation of what is said and done, this neither implies that a given state of affairs is not the case nor indicates that a knowledge of it is impossible. Following Webster, Murray wishes to employ a dialogical methodological model in the critical realist's search for reality and our knowledge of it. We shall return to this proposal shortly.

While this attempt to establish a middle-of-the-road position in relation to the more dominant perspectives on these issues is in itself commendable, it is doomed from the outset because it builds upon the very atomistic presuppositions as the views that it seeks to overcome. In defense of the need to acknowledge the essential difference or gap between cultures in order for one to gain knowledge of the other, Murray quotes Webster as saying, "The gap is the foundation of understanding, not its subversion" (p. 147). Furthermore, in arguing on behalf of critical realism, Webster claims that although both objectivity and subjectivity are merely "reifying abstractions," they nevertheless "are the framework in which an elusive truth must continually be reestablished" (p. 148). The crux of the difficulty here is that this effort to establish a dialogical approach after a dichotomy between the two opposing poles has been established necessarily contains within it the very dualism it seeks to eliminate.

The "gap" of which Webster speaks is actually a twofold dichotomy that goes back as far as Plato but was most clearly focused in the works of such modern philosophers as René Descartes, David Hume, and Immanuel Kant. At one level the gap is posited as existing between the culture of the anthropologist and "other" or "different" cultures, such as that of the American Indian. At a deeper level it is established at the outset between any knowing subject and any object to be known. Plato's choice of visual perception as the metaphor of all knowledge has the epistemic gap between the knower and the known built into it. In like manner, Descartes's affirmation of deductive proof as the standard of cognition places what is to be known outside and independent of the mind of the knower. Hume's skepticism concerning inductive inference and Kant's critique of any attempt to gain knowledge of "the thing itself" are both worked out within the confines dictated by their initial commitment to the dichotomy between subject and object. Thus both critical realism and postmodernism, because they implicitly accept this dichotomy, in actuality represent just one more variation in the long-established intellectual tradition of the West.

The above account of the cognitive "gap," which Murray and others are struggling to overcome, should make it clear that the real difficulty lies with the idea that human beings, whether as knowers or as the known, are fundamentally separate from and independent of one another. This basic "atomism" not only leads to a whole host of moral and sociopolitical confusions, which are beyond the province of this book, but is as well the progenitor of the dilemma facing would-be knowers in general and anthropologists in particular. Once the world, including persons, is conceived of as composed of discrete and self-contained units, the problem of how to bridge the gaps between them through cognition is as inevitable as it is ineradicable. As long as the gap remains, as long as the knower and the known are assumed to be separated from each other, the specter of skepticism will always haunt us, whether in the modernist versions of Hume and Kant or the postmodernist versions of Derrida and Foucault.

A Four-Step Proposal

My own proposal for the avoidance of the sort of dilemma encountered by Murray, and all of us interested in achieving a sound, useful theory of knowledge, involves four essential components. The first pertains to the relationship between the various levels or circles of meaning in linguistic activity. Murray focused his awareness of the difficulties involved here in terms of the poly-significance and contextuality of all language. The central problem is how to keep the open-textured character of language from eroding into sheer relativism and gibberish. Once we acknowledge that what Murray calls the "mediating process between speaker and hearer" does in fact affect the meaning of an utterance, how can we know how much and which part, if any, of the original utterance has been understood?

The first move toward extracting ourselves from this muddle is simply to recognize and affirm that in spite of all the skeptical possibilities and frequent misunderstandings surrounding human discourse, we do in fact manage to understand one another. More pointedly, the very notions and experiences of doubt and misunderstanding are logically dependent on those of successful communication. Within the dualistic parameters set by the Western philosophical tradition, it is easy to overlook the simple truth that at its very center language works; indeed, it must first work in order for break-downs to be possible. We do not begin with doubt in language; rather, we assume at the outset that we have or will be understood. In other words, the notion of multiple meanings is itself parasitic on that of primary meaning in a given context; otherwise language could never be acquired in the first place. Meaningfulness, like human beings, should be considered "innocent" until proven guilty.

What this boils down to is this: the distance or "otherness" between persons and/or cultures that worries Murray so much not only is no different in kind from that which characterizes all human cognition but is not ultimately problematic with regard to the possibility of mutual understanding. Surely a newborn infant stands in a far more precarious situation with respect to grasping the meaning of its natural language than the anthropologist does in grappling with a culture and language markedly different from his or her own. The possibilities of misunderstanding would seem to be nearly infinite for the infant, yet somehow communication quickly and naturally begins to take place, and what Murray terms the "effacement" of the meaning of the original utterances is, in the vast majority of cases, sorted out as it occurs. People, including anthropologists, literary critics, and philosophers, speak both in order to be understood and because they are understood. In short, meaning is already on the scene when any of us arrives; if it were not, we would never come to participate in it, let alone be able to worry about it not working. Moreover, at every level our language presupposes that those to whom we speak or write will in fact ascertain our meaning in spite of the various possibilities for misunderstanding.

Here we might consider the case of irony. In this mode of discourse the speaker says the very opposite of what is meant and does so expecting to be understood. Of course, such understanding may not take place, sometimes with dire consequences, but the fact remains that irony is a very common mode of speech and is generally understood rather easily. Here, too, we may well mention all the variations of what might be called "indirect speech," from simile and allegory through analogy and metaphor, to satire and rhetoric. All of these linguistic patterns are extremely common and effective. Moreover, not only have we, with Murray's help, come to understand better the political manipulation of Indians by white Americans, but we have even understood Derrida's warnings about the myriads of possible mis-understanding. In addition, even the gap between myself the writer and you the reader has, I hope, been bridged by this discussion, even by this very sentence. Michael Polanyi, in his book *Personal Knowledge*, has termed this vectorial character of language, this logical priority of meaningfulness, "universal intent." For him, both in meaning and knowledge, responsible choice enables us to avoid the extremes of dogmatic "objectivism" and skeptical "relativism."

> While compulsion by force or by neurotic obsession excludes responsibility, compulsion by universal intent establishes responsibility. The strain of this responsibility is the greater—other things being equal—the wider the range of alternatives left open to choice and the more conscientious the person responsible for the decision. While the choice in question are given to arbitrary egocentric decisions, a craving for the universal sustains a constructive effort and narrows down this discretion to the point where the agent making the decision finds that he cannot do otherwise. The freedom of the subjective person to do as he pleases is overruled by the freedom of the responsible person to act as he must. (p. 309)

The second component of my proposed solution of Murray's forked-tongue dilemma involves a recognition and exploration of the contextual character of linguistic activity. Even as this dependency on context entails the possibility of multiple meanings and misunderstandings, so it also ensures the possibility of communication and understanding. There are at least three main features of the contextual aspect of linguistic meaning that bear mentioning: the physical, the instrumental, and the social. To begin with the physical, it must be remembered that every utterance takes place within a physical environment that at least in part determines its meaning. This environment includes everything from the immediate material objects and surroundings to the gestures and facial expressions of the speaker.

A statement such as "The door is open" will mean different things when said, say, in an office, on a country side road, or in front of a garage. In the first instance it could mean an invitation to visit the boss; in the second it might convey the encouragement of a friend with whom one is taking a walk; while in the last it may serve as a description. In each case, the hearer relies heavily on his or her tacit awareness of all such considerations when ascertaining the meaning of the utterance. Even a written statement occurs within a physical environment, comprising such things as the sort of document it appears in, the title of the book or essay, the author's name, and the specific words that are printed immediately before and after it. All of these factors figure into one's interaction with what is read, including and perhaps especially the writings of postmodern thinkers. Without relying on these obvious but crucial physical features, it is impossible to discern the difference between significance and insignificance, declaration and irony, or creative wordplay and mere word salad.

There are also instrumental features that help determine the meaning of speech. It is absolutely essential to be able to read the force or thrust of what J. L. Austin refers to as "speech-acts" if one is going to understand a given utterance. The statement "The door is open," when said to a youngster who continually forgets to close the door, may well function as an imperative ("Close the door") rather than as a descriptive utterance, even when the physical factors are identical. It is a fascinating fact that tiny children learn the instrumental value of speech, as it is mediated through intonation, prior to acquiring any real vocabulary. They ask questions, give orders, tell jokes, and so on long before they can say actual words. They carry on conversations with their various toys, talk into play telephones, and contribute to family humor at the dinner table by means of intonation, gesture, and facial expression.

All of these considerations apply equally well to written language. Signs encountered along the roadway provide an interesting example. Traffic signs are read as having a different thrust or purpose than advertisements, for instance. "Buy Gas Here," "Eat," and "Exit" are not taken as imperatives, while "Stop," "Yield," and "Detour" are not read as invitations. Learning to interpret the meaning of these signs is a matter of learning to comprehend the instrumental force of the linguistic context. Most often no instructions are provided. Deciding whether an utterance is ironic or sincere, literal or symbolic, logical or rhetorical is an extremely complicated process requiring years of participation in the dialogical interchange appropriate to any given language level and/or area. The present abstract analysis of the multifaceted character of language is itself a concrete case in point, as are other theoretical forms of writing. Their instrumental aim is clearly different from that of factual or creative writing, and one learns to comprehend this difference by participating in these respective disciplines.

This brings us to the social quality of each and every linguistic context. Although it is obvious enough, it is frequently forgotten that all speech takes place within a social context. This context involves not only the speaker and the hearer, or immediate audience, but the wider speaking community as well. Temporality and spatiality factor into this dynamic very heavily, since all of language has a history and projects toward the future and also carries across or is confined by spatial distance. Most important here, perhaps, is the simple fact that language as a social phenomenon is already present when each of us arrives on the scene. We indwell speech, much as a fish indwells water, until speech comes to indwell us, and by means of language we not only are enculturated into our own society but are endowed with humanity. At one extreme, even Helen Keller described herself as a mere "phantom" who never engaged in an intentional act prior to becoming a member of the speaking community. At the other extreme, even the Aborigines of the Australian outback, whose life was once devoted almost entirely to the task of survival, speak an exceedingly complex and rich language.

The point of the above discussion vis-à-vis Murray's project is that the sort of dialogical model of communication and understanding that he seeks must include a thorough awareness of the main features of the contextual character of all language, both spoken and written. Such an awareness helps dismantle the skeptical implications of relativism and cognitive dualism before they get off the ground. When we affirm the axial and evolutionary center of linguistic activity, the need for an absolute foundation for meaning and truth withers away, along with the specter of skepticism inherent within it. More specifically, the foregoing remarks concerning the social quality of linguistic contexts brings us directly to the third component of my proposed solution to Murray's forked-tongue dilemma. This component centers on the social character of human personhood itself in order to demonstrate the basic inadequacies of the individualism presupposed by realists and relativists alike.

Murray has it right when he affirms the need to focus on the mediators and the mediating process in order to overcome the "effacement" of meaning resulting from the effort to bridge this gap. His dilemma, however, continues to plague him right through the end of his book because he proposes this mediational, dialogical model of communication and knowledge within the parameters already established by the dualistic and atomistic presuppositions of the very paradigm he is seeking to displace. He has arrived on the scene with too little because he has arrived too late. One cannot first assume that speakers and hearers, writers and readers are already separated from each other and then seek to reconnect them by viewing their interrelationships as dialogical. Rather, one must begin by affirming the social, symbiotic character of human life at both the individual and the cognitive levels. Communication and cognition are not ancillary, parasitic aspects of human existence; they are constitutive and regulatory. Thus mistakes and misfires are the exception, not the norm.

Newborn infants come into a social world that is already in full swing, and they come seeking participation in that world. They respond to, imitate, and initiate linguistic activity from, or even before, the day they arrive on the scene. Saying what one means directly and telling the truth are logically prior to all other semiotic transactions, since without being able to assume them, we can neither come to understand irony and linguistic humor nor learn to recognize, let alone tell, a lie. In like manner, at the adult level all utterances and writings emerge within the social intercourse of language and do so because their authors expect to have an effect within the patterns thereof. Once we accredit our reciprocal ability to express and understand meaning linguistically as absolutely axial to the other sphere of human existence, we can set aside the temptation to begin our examination of language, together with linguistic and cultural "effacement," by erecting a chasm of potential misunderstanding between a speaker and hearer(s) or a writer and reader(s).

More specifically, persons themselves are more like currents and eddies in a stream than like islands. Not only are the material and social worlds largely mediated to us through our participation in linguistic interaction, but even the person we are becoming, including our personalities and values, is largely a function of our interactions with other linguistic agents. From parents and siblings, through neighbors and teachers, to friends and public figures, we are constantly being shaped and reshaped though the dialogical mediation of linguistic omnipresence. Thus the highly complex psychological and sociopolitical dynamics involved in Indian speech, along with its translation and representation, as well as those at the heart of postmodern discussion, are also part and parcel of this ongoing, symbiotic interaction by means of which persons as well as issues and perspectives are woven.

The fourth and final component of my proposal for overcoming the postmodern dilemma that Murray focuses on so well speaks directly to the possibility of achieving reliable knowledge of the world by means of mediational dialogue. Murray's concentration on the dialogical character of communication and cognition is certainly a move in the right direction. However, it is essential to speak more specifically to two aspects of the traditional model of knowledge, namely, its intellectualist and its representationist emphasis. When cognition is defined exclusively in terms of mental processes and states, the result is an overly static and abstract caricature of cognitive activity. Space does not permit even a cursory presentation of the case for a more pragmatic task- and body-oriented view of cognition. Suffice it to say that knowledge can no longer be thought of as confined to the processes and states of the mind. By this point it should be clear that we learn and comprehend through interacting with our environment, including other learners, generally in conjunction with some rather specific problem or task.

Likewise, when our understanding of cognition is limited to the mental pictures or propositional representations that we form, we simply reiterate and reinforce the gap between the knower and the known built into the atomistic dualism of Western thought. If we assume that we can represent the world only as independent observers of it, we are essentially cut off from it and necessarily subject to the debilitating effects of relativism and skepticism. The fact is, however, that we are actively and intimately connected to the world by means of our pragmatic and somatic interaction with it. Better yet, we are an integral part of the world, and our understanding of it is itself an aspect of that interaction, which partly constitutes what we call reality. Thus we do not represent the world merely through cognition; we alter and form it, even as we are altered and formed by it.

This completes my fourfold proposal for getting beyond the impasse constructed by the postmodernist exploitation of the deficien-

cies built into the modernist understanding of understanding. It consists of going back to square one and reconceiving the fundamental
nature of our place within the relationship to the world we seek to
know. Unless such a fresh beginning is made, there is no escape from
the cul-de-sac resulting from the conflict between modernism and
postmodernism, between the elusive universalism of "objectivity"
and the persistent relativism of "subjectivity." David Murray's book
Forked Tongues both highlights and suggests the proper dialogical
result of this dilemma. However, in my view, the notion of dialogue
requires a far more radical and thorough implementation if it is to
liberate us from the entanglements of Western dualism.

7

Language and Reality:
The Work of Benjamin Lee Whorf

Chances are that you would be perceiving this sentence quite differently had you been told that it is a coded message of which one is supposed to read only every other word. Or consider the fact that while my wife sees the make and model of nearly any passing car, I am lucky to see its color. In parallel manner, it is common knowledge that whether we experience certain people or events positively or negatively often depends on how they have been described to us beforehand. These simple examples serve well to focus the crucial question of this chapter: does language merely label and describe reality, or does it create and shape it as well?

This aspect of the issues surrounding our concern with the threshold of language shifts the emphasis from questions of cognitivity, as in the previous chapter, to questions of what philosophers call "ontology," or how the world is structured. In anthropological discussions of such issues no name crops up more frequently than that of Benjamin Lee Whorf. Whorf's investigation of this topic, deriving from his studies with Edward Sapir and generally referred to as the "Sapir-Whorf hypothesis," resulted in a philosophical theory alternatively designated "linguistic determinism" or "linguistic relativity." Whorf's view affirms that both our thought patterns and the world we experience are largely a function of the structure of the language we have been enculturated to speak.

On the basis of his outstanding work with Aztec and Mayan languages, as well as his participation in Sapir's classes at Yale, Whorf had already established himself as a linguistic scholar by the time he turned his attention to Native American languages in general and the

Hopi language in particular in the 1930s. He published a number of essays during his lifetime, and others have been published since his death. The most important of these have been collected into a single volume by John B. Carroll under the title *Language, Thought, and Reality*. The following discussion of Whorf's work is based on this collection.

In the early chapters of the present book, we were concerned primarily with the notion of threshold as it pertains to language acquisition on the part of various potential speakers. In the previous chapter, we turned our attention to those aspects of this notion that apply more directly to different forms of cross-cultural communication. In this chapter we will see the notion of threshold relocated, as it were, in relation to the far frontier between human thought and speech, on the one hand, and reality as it is encountered and interacted with, on the other. At the very least, an examination of Whorf's theories will lead us directly to this frontier; at best it may well provide us with helpful insights into the character and function of language.

Whorf's Findings

Beginning with an analysis of verbs in the Hopi language, Whorf draws some conclusions about the implications of verb type and structure for our experience and understanding of the world around us. He notes that Hopi does not formalize the contrast between completed and uncompleted action. Rather, it formalizes different varieties of the contrast between "point-locus" and "extent-locus," such that the inflections or verb endings serve to distinguish the manner of the action rather than whether or not it is completed. Thus the form of the verbs, not the nouns, indicates whether a given line is meandering, zigzagged, serrated, or fringed, and whether a fluid makes one wave or a continuous tossing of waves.

Whorf documents a good number of such verb inflections, each expressing distinguishable vibration patterns. He then concludes that this way of classifying and employing verbs is far more appropriate to the tasks of subatomic physics than is the noun-oriented or object-centered pattern characteristic of Indo-European languages. Here is how he puts it:

All this has a wider interest than the mere illustration of an aspect-form. It is an illustration of how language produces an organization of experience. We are inclined to think of language simply as a technique of expression, and not to realize that language first of all is a classification and arrangement of the stream of sensory experience which results in a certain world order, a certain segment of the world that is easily expressible by the type of symbolic means that language employs. In other words, language does in a cruder but also a broader and more versatile way the same thing that science does. We have just seen how the Hopi language maps out a certain terrain of what might be termed primitive physics. . . . The Hopi aspect-contrast which we have observed, being obligatory upon their verb forms, practically forces the Hopi to notice and observe vibratory phenomena, and further more encourages them to find names for and classify such phenomena. (pp. 55–56)

Whorf expands this analysis of time to include the notion of space. In the Western mind, derived from the Indo-European language patterns, both space and time are essentially independent, static realities, the former three-dimensionally and the latter sequentially so. Newtonian space and time are closed and unidirectional, respectively. The focus of the Hopi, more "Einsteinian" view of reality, as revealed in verb patterns, is on the threshold between reality as realized and reality as expected (as contrasted to past, present, and future). That which is wished or hoped for, wanted or intended, falls under the verb classification that Whorf designates "expective." As he says:

In translating into English, the Hopi will say that these entities in process of causation 'will come' or that they—the Hopi—'will come to' them, but, in their own language, there are no verbs corresponding to our 'come' and 'go' that mean simple and abstract/motion, our purely kinematic concept. The words in this case translated 'come' refer to the process of eventuating without calling it motion—they are 'eventuates to here' (pew'i) or 'eventuates from it' (anggo) or 'arrived' (pitu, pl. oki) which refers only to the terminal manifestation, the actual arrival at a given point, not to any motion preceding it. (p. 60)

One of Whorf's more well-known distinctions is that between "overt" and "covert" grammar. Shifting from Hopi to Navajo, he points out that the latter has a covert classification of the whole world of objects based partly on animation and partly on shape. Inanimate bodies fall into two, or perhaps even more, classes, referred to as "round objects" and "long objects." "The Navajo so-called 'round' and 'long' nouns are not marked in themselves nor by any pronouns. They are marked only in the use of certain very important verb stems, in that a different stem is required for a 'round' or a 'long' subject or object" (p. 70). Extremely subtle aspects of covert grammar, labeled by Whorf as "cryptotypes," may be expressed through certain verbs so as to associate them in ways quite different from our own way of doing so. In Hopi, for instance, "going out" and "going in" are construed as placing a subject within a force field, similar to "falling," "spilling," and "jumping." "According to the logic of Hopi linguists," says, Whorf, "a person about to enter a house or go outdoors launches off and yields himself to a new influence like one who falls or leaps" (p. 73). Clearly, according to Whorf, such ways of classifying verbs carry with them different ways of anticipating and experiencing the world.

Whorf noted that there are verb patterns in Hopi that differentiate (a) actions the starting of which implies there will be a certain amount of actual maintenance invested on the part of the relevant subject thereof from (b) actions that do not and (c) actions wherein the subject is carried along by the activity, even, if need be, without the subject's intent. "Thus 'sleep' is classified here by Hopi as though it felt sleep to be a state which the subject developed into by a continuous readjustment, not one by which he launched himself into; while 'running' and 'talking' are regarded as states launched into, not progressed or adjusted into" (p. 108). "Falling" or "spilling," on the other hand, are neither progressed nor launched into.

At one point (pp. 113–14) Whorf discusses the three different verb patterns used to make assertions, each having its own form of validity, as it were. First, there is the "reportive," the simple stating of the fact or event. Next, there is the "expective," which declares an anticipation on the part of the speaker concerning the fact or event, even though it has already taken place. These "tense" patterns are more determinative of perspective or posture than they are of time, which is quite unlike the tense patterns in Indo-European languages. Third, what Whorf calls the "nomic" patterns offers the statement as a general truth, as affirming a general, ongoing condition rather than an act or event. The differences among these "tenses" must be determined contextually. Whorf gives the following example:

> Thus to the Hopi 'he is running' need not be different from 'he was running,' for, if both the speaker and listener can see the runner, than the 'is' of the former sentence means merely that the listener can see for himself what he is being told; he is being given redundant information, and this is the only difference from the latter sentence. (p. 114)

In addition to his studies with Edward Sapir, the work of Fabre d'Olivet (1768–1825) exerted a strong influence on Whorf's approach to the relation between language and reality. D'Olivet was seen by Whorf as establishing the psycholinguistic basis of speech, especially as revealed in prefixes and suffixes and in vowel patterns. For him such syntactic phenomena were not merely arbitrary sound patterns but deeply embedded semantic symbols, arising out of onomatopoeic roots. D'Olivet saw these etymological patterns as embodying concurrent or even identical meaning. For instance, the appearance of the phoneme "fl" at the front of such terms as "flash," "flicker," "fly," and "flame," or "cl" at the beginning of "clash," "click," "climb," and "clatter," is viewed as unaccidental (p. 75). D'Olivet also spoke of this merger of symbol and meaning as being grounded in our embodied behavior, perhaps as a kind of gesture. As yet another example of how different linguistic patterns factor into or help to constitute our reality, Whorf mentions the peculiar and dangerous practice of designating as "empty" gasoline drums that no longer contain liquid gas.

> Thus, around a storage of what are called 'gasoline drums,' behavior will tend to be a certain type, that is, great care fill be exercised; while around a storage of what are called 'empty gasoline drums,' it will tend to be different—careless, with little repression of smoking or of tossing cigarette stubs about. Yet the 'empty' drums are perhaps the more dangerous, since they contain explosive vapor. Physically the situation is hazardous, but the linguistic analysis according to regular analogy must employ the word 'empty,' which inevitably suggests lack of hazard. (p. 135)

In like fashion, Whorf calls attention to the differences between the English and Hopi ways of speaking of, and thus construing, plural numbers. In English we count any and each aspect of reality, no matter how diverse, "objectively" or abstractly. Thus both a number of physical objects and a number of days are spoken of similarly, even though the latter can never be encountered directly, as a group. Thus time, like objects, tends to become quantified and static in our experience. Whorf contrasts this with Hopi:

> In Hopi there is a different linguistic situation. Plurals and cardinals are used only for entities that form or can form an objective group. There are no imaginary plurals, but instead ordinals used with singulars. Such an expression as 'ten days' is not used. The equivalent statement is an operational one that reaches one day by a suitable count. 'They stayed ten days' becomes 'they stayed until the eleventh day' or 'they left after the tenth day.' (p. 140)

This same pattern obtains in Hopi with regard to the cycles of the days and/or seasons. In Hopi these designations are never given nominative, or objective, status, as in the English "summer is hot" or "this summer." Rather, they function more as adverbs, deriving their meaning from a current event or action, by modifying verbs, instead of the other way around (p. 143). Overall, the main contrast that Whorf wished to make between Hopi and Indo-European languages is that while the latter largely construes reality by means of nouns, as the labels for "persons, places, or things," thereby atomizing the world, the former construes reality by means of verbs, thus emphasizing the interactive and process character of the world (p. 147).

The result of these crucially different construal patterns, according to Whorf, is that such basic notions as time, space, and individuation are lived out quite differently at the respective behavioral levels. The Hopi discernment of time as flowing duration undifferentiated by arbitrary divisions between past, present, and future, for instance, results in a characteristic emphasis on preparation.

> This includes announcing and getting ready for events well beforehand, elaborate precautions to insure persistence of desired conditions, and stress on good will as the prepare of right results. . . . The Hopi deal with the future by working within a present situation which is expected to carry impress, both obvious and occult, forward into the future event of interest. (p. 148)

Whorf suggests that these different views of time go hand-in-hand with the fact that the western European tradition values historical concerns, such as tracing individual causal connections and record-keeping, while the Hopi have little use for such things, since for them the past and future are in an experiential sense fully and always present (p. 153). Similarly, Whorf hypothesizes that the Western tendency to derive nonspatial perceptual categories from spatial or visual ones contributes to our proclivity for rapid and highly differentiated bodily movement, as if we were dividing space up into objective units, a phenomenon largely absent from Hopi behavioral patterns (p. 155).

Yet another example of the way, according to Whorf, that language and reality-as-experienced are inextricably intertwined can be seen in the absence of a term for room in the Hopi tongue. Even though they are a pueblo people and live in what would appear to us to be apartment-like structures, the Hopi have a word for house but not for room. The term that is generally translated as room in English more correctly indicates a location within the spatial or relational behavior of people.

> They are not set up as entities that can function in a sentence like terms for people, animals, or masses of matter having characteristic form, or again, human groups and animal relations, but are treated as PURELY RELATION CONCEPTS, of an adverbial type. Thus hollow spaces like room, chamber, hall, are not really NAMED as objects are, but are rather located; i.e., positions of other things are specified so as to show their location in such hollow spaces. (p. 202)

Along these same lines, Whorf mentions the fact that within Hopi culture ceremony and ritual are the primary social "institutions" and these are defined for them, unlike for ourselves, in terms of activities and events. Thus the Hopi do not think of reality in terms of structures and entities but in terms of relationships and processes. This difference even extends to the fact that in Hopi there is no term for the kiva as a "room" per se, even though it stands at the very center of religious and social life. For the Hopi the kiva is more of a locus of activity, an intersection of patterns, than it is a thing or room enclosed by walls (p. 205).

One of the passages in which Whorf most directly states the central claim he is making is the following:

> We dissect nature along lines laid down by our native languages. The categories and types that we isolate from the world of phenomena we

do not find there because they stare every observer in the face; on the contrary, the world is presented in a kaleidoscope flux of impressions which has to be organized by our minds—and this means largely by the linguistic systems in our minds. We cut nature up, organize it into concepts, and ascribe significance as we do, largely because we are parties to an agreement to organize it in this way—an agreement that holds throughout our speech community and is codified in the patterns of our language. (p. 212–13)

Whorf backs this hypothesis up with the fact that the Hopi language describes everything that flies as one of two classifications, birds and other things. The Hopi actually refer to insects, airplanes, and aviators all by the same word. If this seems like too large a class to be useful, consider the Eskimo, who have no noun term for snow as such but have multitudes of verb inflections by which to designate the many variations of that which universally characterizes their environment. They would find our half-dozen or so distinctions hopelessly vague and inadequate for survival. At the other end of the spectrum, Whorf mentions the Aztec, who have but one term for snow, ice, and cold as a group; "ice" is the noun form, "cold" is the adjectival form, and snow is called "ice mist" (p. 216).

A final conclusion that Whorf draws from his study of Native American languages and cultures is that not only do different languages construe the world differently, but because of this some languages are more useful for specific tasks or fields of endeavor than others. More pointedly, he claims that Hopi, with its event (verb) and process-oriented structure, is better suited to quantum physics than are Indo-European languages. Whorf reasons that the latter's predilection for the subject-predicate linguistic format, together with its overly strong emphasis on nouns, requires a static conceptual framework even when one is trying to speak about a reality that is fundamentally composed of organized energy in motion (pp. 237–41).

More than once Whorf alludes to the invention of non-Euclidean geometries as a classic example of the sort of theory he is promoting. A little over a century ago, it was commonly assumed by mathematicians and philosophers alike that the laws of Euclid's geometry applied to the entire universe. With the availability of non-Euclidean systems, however, it has now become apparent that there are many ways of slicing up the spatial pie, each being "true" in the sense of being internally consistent. In fact, as a result of Einstein's work, it has turned out that one of these "new" geometries works better than the others, including Euclid's, in relation to outer space. Whorf sees different languages as parallel to these different geometries in general, and Hopi in particular as more parallel to Einstein's universe than Indo-European tongues.

Philosophers, Language, and Reality

Whorf's theory of the relation between language and reality—that the former largely constitutes the latter—relates to the history of Western philosophy at a number of junctures. By examining several of these intersections, we may be able to clarify more precisely the main contours of Whorf's overall position and gain a better idea of what he is and is not saying. In addition, perhaps some potential corroboration or criticism can be found among the insights and emphases of other thinkers.

The traditional Western understanding of the relationship between language and reality is rooted at least as far back as Plato's theory of "Forms." Plato reasoned that in order for language and thought to have any meaning, the terms we use must ultimately refer to abstract definitions or concepts called "Forms" or "Ideas," under which all the entities or qualities designated thereby can be subsumed. Otherwise we would never be able to know whether or not we were talking about the same things. Thus, whenever we use the term "horse," it must refer in the primary sense to the ideal, abstract concept of "horseness" and only secondarily to the various animals denoted thereby. In his dialogue *The Sophist* (259d–260d), Plato employs the metaphor of weaving to explain how language thus blends and interlaces the various Forms by way of conveying ideas and information.

Like most European thinkers after him, Plato gave no serious attention to the possibility of different languages having radically different structures and thereby perhaps entailing appropriately different conceptual realities. Thus we can see that Whorf's approach to this whole question, based as it is in a firsthand knowledge of various languages that are quite distinct in structure, is in conflict with that of Plato in particular and the history of Western thought in general. For Plato and the standard Western view, language is ultimately based on reality, whereas for Whorf the relationship is at least reciprocal or symbiotic and perhaps even reversed; that is, reality may in fact be entirely a function of language.

In one form or another the basic thrust of Plato's view predominated in the West throughout the centuries well into modern times. In the writings of John Locke, it was given a psychological interpretation, for he construed language as providing the names or symbols for the ideas, or "objects of thought," that sensory experience deposits in the human mind (*Essay Concerning Human Understanding,* book 2, chapter 1). These ideas are themselves, in turn, copies of the various objects and qualities in the physical world that impress themselves on our senses. Thus for Locke, words stand for ideas that are themselves representations of things in reality. Once again we can see that the vector here is unilateral, from reality through the mind to language. Although Whorf does not develop his line of thought within a psychological framework, he can be interpreted as affirming the very opposite of Locke. For he presumably argues that the distinct structure and character of language itself create or shape the mental ideas that we in turn project onto the world. Locke, along with nearly all other modern philosophers, clearly views language as representing or standing for ideas or thoughts, as well as secondarily for the objects and qualities comprising the world. Whorf, on the other hand, views language as in some sense forming our concepts and through them shaping our world.

Bishop George Berkeley, in many ways a follower of Locke's empiricism, actually departs from the traditional view of language and reality by offering a far more sophisticated understanding of the relationship between them. Berkeley acknowledges that language has several important functions in addition to that of representation and that most terms have more than a single signification (*Principles of Human Knowledge,* introduction #18–20). Although Whorf himself does not have much to say about the nonrepresentational functions of language, it seems clear that this broader perspective on the polysignificant character of speech would be more in harmony with Whorf's perspective than were the views of Plato, Locke, and others. Unfortunately, once he began to develop the content of his philosophy, Berkeley managed to ignore or contravene his more revolutionary introductory insights. But that is a story for another time.

It is in the philosophy of Immanuel Kant that we first encounter a thinker whose thoughts about language and reality begin to mesh with those of Whorf. In developing what he called his "Copernican Revolution" in philosophy, Kant maintained that the experience upon which all our knowledge is based is itself a composite of the interaction between our sensory input and the structure of our minds. Unlike the empiricists, Kant argued that the "categories of our understanding," such as space, time, and causation, filter and shape the data of sensation as they come into the mind. Thus, what we know is a function of the interaction between our encounter with the things comprising the world and our human modes of thought. Kant concluded as well that since what we know is necessarily structured by the categories of the understanding, it is futile, indeed meaningless, to seek knowledge about the world in and of itself, independent of our cognitive interaction with it (*Critique of Pure Reason,* preface to second edition). Such metaphysical efforts are, by definition, doomed from the outset, since we cannot know what lies beyond our experience. The categorical structure of our mind provides the very condition upon which experience as we know it is itself possible, and therefore it makes no sense to seek knowledge outside this condition.

By shifting at least part of the basis of knowledge and experience from the external world to the structure of the mind, Kant clearly moved away from the received Western tradition and closer to Whorf's view. Whorf, too, maintained that at least to a large degree our minds shape the world we live in and it makes no sense to talk about the world as it is, in and of itself, apart from our interactions in and with it. In addition, of course, Whorf contended that it is our enculturation into language that shapes the structure of our world-shaping minds. It is doubtful whether Kant would have followed Whorf in this regard because, he, like his contemporaries and predecessors, was ignorant of or simply ignored the possibility of radically different natural languages giving rise to quite diverse ways of thinking about and thus encountering the world. For Kant, the categories of understanding are the same for all peoples, while for Whorf it is clear that they are not.

The presuppositions inherent within the standard Western approach to the relation between language and reality only really came to the foreground in the twentieth century. The logical empiricism developed by Bertrand Russell and the young Ludwig Wittgenstein, often dubbed "logical atomism," focused attention for the first time on the nature of language itself. In his brilliant and highly influential *Tractatus Logico-Philosophicus,* Wittgenstein propounded the "picture theory of meaning," according to which language is supposed to duplicate the factual arrangements in the world in its own logico-grammatical structure. The degree of correspondence between language and reality is thus the criterion of both meaning and truth. Any utterances that do not actually mirror physical states of affairs were said to be meaningless: "What can be said at all can be said clearly, and what we cannot talk about we must consign to silence" (preface).

This theory, sometimes referred to as the "luggage-tag" or "naming" theory of language, construes language as a passive and static representation or reality, a second-order or parasitic phenomenon that can only and always reflect how things are. Clearly, this view is the polar opposite of Whorf's view, whether one gives the latter a weak or a strong interpretation. Some theorists see this "picture theory of meaning" as a linguistic version of Kant's philosophy, wherein the categories of the understanding are transplanted into the depth-grammar of linguistic activity. However, Kant's insight into the interactive character of the relation between mind and the world in creating our experienced reality was clearly left out of the early Wittgenstein's philosophy of language.

After a hiatus of some fifteen years, Wittgenstein returned to philosophy and completely revamped his approach to the question of meaning. In his mature work, *Philosophical Investigations,* Wittgenstein maintained that language is far more multifarious than the entire Western tradition had ever imagined. He argued that the meaning of an utterance is a function of the use to which it is put within a specific physical and social context. In addition to providing descriptions or "pictures" of states of affairs, language is now acknowledged to be a medium for asking questions, telling stories, giving orders, expressing feelings, making lists, solving problems, forming and testing theories, and so on (see *Philosophical Investigations,* #23).

Within this understanding of language there is the possibility of making room for the more creative or "orphic" function that Whorf spoke of. For the later Wittgenstein, not only does language fulfill many diverse functions, but its various patterns and purposes, which Wittgenstein termed "language games," are constantly evolving.

Moreover, since speech arises and evolves within the context of our mutual interaction with the environment, it helps to shape the world as much as it is shaped by it. In short, for Wittgenstein the relationship between language and reality is extremely organic and fluid. As human needs and aspirations change, so language and behavior change, thereby altering the nature of the social and physical context within which we live. In a very real sense we create "corporations," "chicks," "communists," and "stress" as much as we encounter them.

More pointedly, by means of our linguistic and related behavioral activity we can be said to create the physical realities of science as much as we "discover" them. Thomas Kuhn's revolutionary *The Structure of Scientific Revolutions,* together with the intense and lengthy discussion stimulated thereby, bears witness to the degree to which it makes sense to speak of our reality as linguistically constituted. The classic case of the dual yet paradoxical character of light, as both continuous and discontinuous, is only one instance of the sort of reciprocity between language and reality that Whorf seemed to have in mind.

Another way to make this point is in terms of Werner Heisenberg's "principle of indeterminacy." As a physicist, Heisenberg came to the conclusion that it is in principle impossible to ascertain both the position and the velocity of any subatomic phenomena, since the medium for such ascertainment must inevitably be light itself. Because every measurement made with light employs the same medium as that of whatever being measured consists, it is impossible to measure such phenomena without altering either their position or velocity or both. Thus, according to Heisenberg, the nature of the reality we know is at least in part determined by the very act of knowing itself.

To be sure, not all of this follows from Wittgenstein's later philosophy of language, but his pragmatic and open-textured character of language to which he called attention surely moves us away from the narrow representationalist view and toward the more creative or constitutivist view urged by Whorf. Wittgenstein himself comes extremely close to Whorf's theory when he speaks of the symbiotic relationship between the act of measuring and the results of measuring:

> If language is to be a means of communication there must be agreement not only in definitions but also (queer as this may sound) in judg-

ments. This seems to abolish logic, but does not do so. It is one thing to describe methods of measurement, and another to obtain and state results of measurement. But what we call "measuring" is partly determined by a certain constancy in results of measurement. (#242)

A thinker who was strongly influenced by Wittgenstein, J. L. Austin, is credited with calling attention to the creative effect of language on reality by means of his analysis of "performative utterances" and his theory of "speech acts." Austin pointed out that when, for instance, we say "I apologize" or "I pronounce you husband and wife" or "I promise," we are in fact performing deeds and thereby altering the world, as well as uttering words. Austin went on, in his *How to Do Things with Words,* to suggest that every utterance can be said to comprise three forces or dimensions, namely, (1) the locutionary (the act of uttering the given words), (2) the illocutionary (the purpose or intent in uttering them), and (3) the perlocutionary (the results achieved by uttering them). Thus, according to Austin, the meaning of any utterance is a function of all three of the forces comprising the total "speech-act." Moreover, his insights into the perlocutionary effect of all speech-acts runs parallel to Whorf's emphasis on the way in which language can construe and even structure our experienced reality.

Moving over to the phenomenological current within contemporary philosophy of language, we can discover emphases that parallel those of Whorf as well. Throughout his work Martin Heidegger emphasized the importance of etymology in seeking to understand the relation between language and reality. He continually strove to cast light on such notions as "truth," for instance, by reminding us that in ancient Greek the word (*aléthia*) literally means "uncovered." In his final years Heidegger shifted his emphasis to the more indirect language of poetry as the more reliable means of allowing reality, or being, to reveal itself. Eventually he retreated into a preference for silence, a move that would not seem to be in harmony with Whorf's approach.

Likewise, Hans-Georg Gadamer, in his *Philosophical Hermeneutics,* has stressed the social and gamelike character of language as the medium by means of which we weave and pattern our existence. His approach is not unlike that of the later Wittgenstein, although he works it out within the framework provided by a more traditional European perspective. Nevertheless, Gadamer strikes a posture that parallels Whorf's in that he clearly stresses the constitutive function of language in relation to reality. Gadamer argues that language is neither arbitrary nor optional, like a tool, but is the medium in which we live and move and have our being. "In all our knowledge of ourselves and in all knowledge of the world, we are always already encompassed by the language that is our own" (pp. 62–63).

Perhaps the European thinker who opens up the most potential points of contact with the views of Whorf is Maurice Merleau-Ponty. In his monumental *Phenomenology of Perception,* Merleau-Ponty takes a stand against the Western philosophical tradition's overwhelming bias in favor of construing knowledge as a function of disembodied minds. He argues that it is by means of our embodiment that we humans enter into and gain purchase in the physical and social worlds. Accordingly, Merleau-Ponty maintains that primordially language must be understood as grounded in bodily functions and activity and not as ancillary to them. More specifically, he traces linguistic meaning to gesture and onomatopoeia as the warp and weft out of which both language and experienced reality are woven and patterned (part 1, chapter 6).

Although he does not stress the somatic and behavioral dimensions of his theory about the constitutive character of languages' relation to reality, Whorf would surely acknowledge their importance. In nearly all the examples presented in the first section of the present chapter, it is evident that Whorf viewed language as arising from human bodily interaction with the environment, both physical and social. Indeed, it would be fair to say that Whorf maintained that both thought and reality are mediated in and through language, which in turn functions as a kind of extension of our embodied intentions and reciprocity. Eventually the ins and outs of such embodied social interaction find their way into the depth-grammar of a people's language and thereby constitute the contours of their particular worldview.

Finally, let me mention one American philosopher whose views on the relation between language and reality have become quite influential and rather controversial. Nelson Goodman, in his book *Ways of Worldmaking,* argues straightforwardly for a constitutivist position. That is to say, he maintains that we create the diverse and overlapping worlds that we inhabit by means of our social, interactive linguistic activity. Goodman acknowledges that there is more to reality than just our various social and linguistic behavior, that we do not simply create our world(s) willy-nilly out of thin air. But he insists that this "more" is experienced as real only in and through our mutual interaction. Therefore it is accurate to say that reality is, ultimately, linguistically constituted.

Goodman specifies that our experienced reality is composed of a wide variety of linguistically constituted worlds, such as those of everyday, physical objects, social roles and groups, religion, art, physics, economics, history, sports, romance, music, ad infinitum. Moreover, he does not think that any and all suggested worlds can or should be legitimized. Each world must establish itself as fruitful within the push-and-pull of human intercourse, with some proving to be more useful for more people over the long haul than others, and some being rejected and forgotten altogether. Goodman says that this is relativism, to be sure, but relativism with rigor (p. 94).

It is not difficult to see that Goodman's "rigorous relativism" is extremely compatible with the linguistic constitutivism of Whorf; both Goodman and Whorf strongly affirm the crucial role of language in the formulation and experience of reality. Perhaps it is helpful to characterize their commonality in terms of the shared emphasis on the mediational function of language, both in creating and shaping reality, on the one hand, and in experiencing and cognizing, on the other. In short, the world as we come to know it, in both its physical and social dimensions, is given to and encountered by us within a linguistic medium that cannot be stripped away or factored out. Speech and the world are thus symbiotically related.

Toward a Resolution

Before reflecting more directly on the issue that Whorf's work has raised concerning the relation between language and reality, let me offer two caveats. First, it should be clear that the question here is not about what can, in one way or another, be said in a given natural language. Linguists have firmly established, and Whorf well knew, that whatever can be said in one language can potentially be said in any other. Whatever human beings find it necessary or useful to say, they will eventually find a way to say in another language. What is "lost" in translation, when such is the case, is nuance or efficiency, not information or insight.

Second, it is perfectly obvious that to some degree language influences or colors the character of reality as we experience it. Everyone will admit this. However, it is equally obvious that exactly how and how much this influence is involved may always, by the nature of the case, remain unknowable. By the time we are able to formulate and investigate the issue at hand, we are already inextricably woven within the fabric of experience of which language constitutes the warp and reality, whatever that means, comprises the weft. "Reality" and "language" are, indeed, themselves the products of conceptual and linguistic activity, so we must operate within them. It is of little use, and may actually make no sense, to lament the limitations of language vis-à-vis reality, since even this lament must be expressed in language.

Two pieces of empirical data tend to corroborate Whorf's claims. First, researcher Linda Rogers conducted an experiment in which she told the same story first in English and then in Navajo to bilingual children while recording their brain-wave patterns (see "Hemisphere Specialization in Language"). When the story was told in English, the left hemisphere of the children's brains was active and the right hemisphere was inactive. When the story was told in Navajo, the situation was reversed. This would seem to indicate that while English, as a noun-centered, subject-predicate-patterned Indo-European language, is processed by the brain's left hemisphere, a verb-centered, event-oriented language like Navajo is processed by the brain's right hemisphere. The "logics" of the two hemispheres are generally held by scientists to follow informational-sequential and spatial-relational patterns, respectively.

Secondly, a clinician working with patients suffering from aphasia recounts explaining to students a patient's inability to group objects in the room into a set or category, even after being given an example and a label, such as "chair." The students found it difficult to understand how a person could grasp the concept of a single object but resort to gazing around the room in confusion when asked to identify other chairs directly in front of them. The teacher informed them that there are Native American languages that group things according to shape rather than function, such that, for instance, a tent peg, a mushroom, and a bird standing on the ground are all designated by the same term. After giving students the term for this classificatory grouping, the teacher asked them to indicate some other members of the set located in the room. Immediately the students began to gaze around the room in confusion quite similar to that of the aphasic patient. Clearly, different language patterns account for the difference in perceptions in such cases (Laura Lee, "Some Semantic Goals for Aphasia Therapy").

It may prove helpful to present the different theoretic possibilities with regard to this issue, arranged along a continuum. At one extreme stand those who would argue that reality is what it is, irrespective of our various human views of it. In short, reality exists independent of whatever perspectives we may hold on it. We may call this position "nonperspectivism." At the other extreme stand those who would maintain that reality is entirely a function of the way we talk and think about it. Let us call this sort of linguistic relativism "hard perspectivism." In between these extremes we might be able to carve out a position whereby we can affirm that while the perspective inherent within a given language structure strongly influences the character of reality, especially as we experience and know it, it is also true that in and by using any given language, a person or society intends to speak of reality as it is or would be if all perceptions could be unified. We might call this position "soft perspectivism."

If we grant that some such position as soft perspectivism is the more desirable, we can further subdivide it into two emphases that are both necessary without either being sufficient in and of itself. One of these emphases is concerned with preserving the objective character of reality such that in some sense it exists as more than, if not independent of, our creative linguistic efforts. After all, the physical world cannot be reconstituted or altered at will. This position is sometimes labeled "critical realism." The other emphasis seeks to preserve the "orphic" quality of language, stressing its constitutive or formative power in relation to experienced reality without denying what might be called the intractable or stubborn aspects of physical reality lying beyond our control. We might call this position "creative realism," and it would seem that this is the view that Whorf's approach best fits under.

Although it is indeed paradoxical to affirm both of these emphases simultaneously, I believe it is necessary to do so in order to take into account the genuine insights each offers into the relation between language and reality. It simply is the case both that the latter is largely formed by the former and that it is not entirely so formed. Moreover, it is not possible, either empirically or conceptually, to determine the extent of mutual interaction between the two, since such determinations will always themselves be part of this linguistic-experiential interaction.

Perhaps one way to ease, if not resolve, the tension generated by this paradox is to conceive of the notion of reality itself as an example of what Kant called a "regulative idea" rather than a "substantive idea." That is to say, the notion of reality as existing independently of our linguistic and cognitive activity can be seen as serving the function of reminding us that the world is always capable of revealing further unanticipated aspects of itself and that human knowledge is never going to be infallible. Thus this notion of independent reality can be said to "regulate" or monitor our cognitive activity without actually contributing to it materially or substantively. In short, no one can ever claim to have exhaustively or completely accurately comprehended reality. This way of putting the matter allows us to acknowledge the intractable and/or inexhaustible nature of reality, and thus in some sense its "independent" existence, while at the same time affirming the constitutive influence of our linguistic and conceptual interaction with it.

Against this conceptual background I would like now to introduce an image offered by Merleau-Ponty that for me sheds a good deal of light on our subject. In the preface to his *Phenomenology of Perception,* Merleau-Ponty takes a stand between an objectivism that would see human cognition as being able to bypass language in its grasp of reality and a subjectivism that would claim that since language necessarily operates between us and reality, no real knowledge is possible at all. He acknowledges that indeed we are inevitably and invariably tied to reality by the "threads" of our intentional activity toward it, including and especially language. Therefore we can never hope to obtain an objective understanding of reality in and of itself. At the same time, however, Merleau-Ponty affirms that we can gain mediated or indirect knowledge of reality by "slackening" the linguistic and cognitive threads by means of which we interact with the world.

This image of "slackening the threads" of our connection to reality suggests the possibility of coming to understand ourselves and the world, as well as our own cognitive and linguistic powers, through and as we engage in interaction, even as we can gain knowledge of the road, the car's steering mechanism, and our own driving skills by paying attention to the vibrations and "play" in the steering wheel as we drive a car—or, to harken back to yesterday, as we can acquire understanding of the horses, the wagon, and our own skills through slackening the reins by which we drive the buckboard, even as we do so. Thus, although we can never disengage ourselves from the factors constituting the symbiotic character of our relation to the world in order to gain an objective, "God's-eye view" of them, neither are we doomed to never knowing anything about them. By slackening these mediating factors even as we employ them, we can gain insight into them, ourselves, and reality.

This way of putting the matter fits rather well with the view expounded by Benjamin Lee Whorf. Not only does it preserve, as he sought to do, the relative stability of the world while affirming the formative power of language, but it reflects the fact that Whorf himself made use of language in a "realist" manner, even as he sought to establish a constitutivist point of view. Throughout his presentation and discussion of the salient linguistic differences between and among various Native American and Indo-European languages, Whorf relies on our understanding of his explanations in English by way of helping us to understand the nuances of Hopi, Navajo, and Shawnee. Thus, although something may be "lost in the translation," a great deal is gained as well. This symbiotic process exemplified by Whorf's efforts serves to underline both the necessity and productivity of treating the relation between language and reality as an interactive one. His seemingly paradoxical procedure is, in fact, merely an example of "slackening" the threads of our cognitivity.

8

A Point of Departure

Generally speaking, a conclusion is not entitled "A Point of Departure." In the case of certain perennial human mysteries, however, such a combination seems extremely appropriate. The mystery of language is, in my view, one such case. For, after all is said and done about what language is and how it is acquired, its fundamentally paradoxical character remains unaltered. Put bluntly, the paradox of language is that it seems impossible, since one must already possess it in order to acquire it. To put it differently, the threshold of language appears to be imperceptible! Even though it is perfectly clear that some animals and nearly all humans move across this threshold into speech, it is equally clear that when and how they do this remains essentially unclear.

The sorts of explorations described in the chapters comprising this book provide us with a great deal of relevant information and insight as to the location and character of this threshold. While such contributions may serve to "hedge in" some of the contents of the threshold of language, it must be acknowledged that at best they do little more than provide a useful point of departure for further explorations and reflections. By way of solidifying such a foothold, I would like to review and briefly expand on the major themes that have emerged from the discussions presented in the foregoing chapters. Then I shall round off this summary by introducing a metaphorical image that seems to me to integrate the important factors and insights involved in a sound appreciation of the familiar mystery that is language. The image I have in mind is that of dance.

Perhaps the best place to begin is with the thoroughly embodied character of human experience and speech. Traditional philosophy has systematically ignored the role of the physical dimension in human cognitive activity, including its linguistic aspect. Knowing and thinking are generally held to be exclusively matters of the mind, with language being simply the external symbolization thereof. If any single truth has emerged from the investigations discussed in this book, it is that this intellectualist perspective is entirely wrong-headed, or better, entirely out of touch with the facts concerning human cognition and speech. It is clear that those who come to know their way around in their mother tongue, both in understanding and expression, do so by means of bodily action and interaction. In addition to the physical aspects of hearing and speaking being crucial to such knowledge, the actual grasping of the dynamics of thought and language is mediated in and through the axis provided by the embodied character of human existence.

Beginning at birth, and most likely well before, an infant's physical movements are patterned so as to actually seek meaningful interaction and significance in the world around it. Not only does an infant arrive on the scene sucking, grasping, and wiggling, but these activities are not random, as one might suppose. In addition to the fact that when spoken to, an infant focuses its eyes on the speaker's eyes rather than the mouth, it has also been established that infants learn after only a few days to distinguish their mother's face from other human faces, and human faces from artificial ones. Even more significantly, the movements of two-month-old infants' hands and feet have been shown to coordinate with the rhythm of the speech and bodily movements of the adult humans caring for them. This reciprocal, interactive embodiment forms the warp and weft out of which human relationship is woven, and this fabric, in turn, provides the matrix from which communication emerges.

Tickling with both fingers and breath and singing and playing primitive versions of "pattycake" soon become the chief media of communication between infants and nurturers. Such activities quickly evolve into simple games, with distinctive rhythms and patterns of their own. In addition, it is important to take note of the degree to which adults alter their speech when speaking to infants, commonly called "baby talk," and of the percentage of this speech that takes an interrogative form. Infants are spoken to as if they already understand language and can answer questions. Moreover, it is perfectly clear that if they are not spoken to as if they understand, they never come to understand. In short, we do not wait around until they understand speech before we engage them in conversation.

It is the cruciality of this embodied character of human existence for the phenomenon of speech that Maurice Merleau-Ponty stressed so heavily in his work. In this view the body serves as the axis point from which extend the intentional threads that tie us to the physical and social world comprising our reality. The commonality of this embodiment, shared in by all human beings, he termed "the flesh" of the world. Michael Polanyi saw our embodiment as the fulcrum from which we engage the world by "dwelling" in its subsidiary particulars in order to know and shape it through speech. Ludwig Wittgenstein, too, stressed the basic behavioral vector that carries and interprets human linguistic activity and meaning. "Speech-acts," to use J. L. Austin's term, are embodied deeds that actually perform and accomplish specific tasks on the physical as well as the social world. The explorations of the preceding chapters demonstrate the significance of this emphasis on embodiment.

A second major theme emerging from the preceding explorations is that of reciprocity. As we indicated in the immediately foregoing pages, the potential member of the speaking community is from the outset surrounded by those belonging to this community, who talk to it incessantly. Moreover, these speakers speak to the infant as if it is already a member of the community. In this way they invite, indeed, they envelop, the potential speaker into language. From initial fondling and tickling, through songs and face making, to hand games and questions, an infant is literally incorporated into the speaking community. That is to say, by means of bodily interaction the potential speaker becomes a part of the body of speakers. In a sense, crossing the threshold of language constitutes a rite of passage, perhaps the rite of passage for becoming a full human being. Like all rites of passage, this "ritual" is grounded in reciprocal human interaction based on established and supervised patterns of speech and behavior.

The necessity of this social reciprocity for becoming a member of the speaking community is cleanly and amply exemplified in the various situations and cases examined in the previous chapters. From the work with chimpanzees and feral children, through the success of Helen Keller and that of normal language acquisitions, to the translation and interpretation of Native American speech, the cruciality of human reciprocity is fully evident. When and only when a potential member of the speaking community is placed within a social context where other persons talk to and expect him or her to talk as well will this person cross the threshold of language. Put the other way around, those who are isolated from or otherwise deprived of linguistic interaction will fail to acquire or develop both linguistically and humanly. At best they will lead a sort of satellite or shadow existence on the fringe of the human community, while at worst they will function as nothing more than like domesticated animals.

These observations also dovetail nicely with the emphasis of the philosophers whose views have been invoked throughout the various stages of our overall study in this book. The social extension of human embodiment is a dominant theme in the works of Merleau-Ponty, Polanyi, and Wittgenstein alike. Moreover, the insights of George Herbert Mead and Nelson Goodman concerning the social character of the basis of selfhood and reality equally call attention to the important role of reciprocity. In a very real sense, we "conjure up" the worlds in which we live, our experienced reality, by means of our linguistic interaction with each other and the natural environment. In a word, both human selfhood and the worlds within which we mutually live are linguistically constituted. Language is that "in which we live, move, and have our being."

A third and very closely related theme emerging from our investigations pertains to the task-oriented quality of language acquisition. Much of, if not most, human social reciprocity and linguistic activity centers around the performance and accomplishment of specific and shared tasks. People do not, except on rare occasions, talk in what might be called a social or physical vacuum. In by far the majority of instances, people speak in order to alter their environment in some way, whether physically, emotionally, or conceptually. Thus the learning of language generally takes place in a pragmatic context, associated inextricably with getting certain things done. In all the sorts of cases investigated in the preceding chapters the degree of success in the understanding of language, whether in acquisition or comprehension, was directly proportionate to the knower's involvement with certain tasks taken up by the members of the speaking community. Usually such tasks were of an everyday, mundane variety centering around the daily needs of eating, sleeping, dressing, running errands, and the like. Eventually, for those who become fully enveloped by language, these tasks evolve into more complex ones, involving human feelings, decisions, attitudes, and policies.

It was this pragmatic quality of human speech that Wittgenstein sought to underscore by his emphasis on linguistic meaning being a function of use in context. As he said, it is extremely helpful to "think of language as a tool." In like manner, J. L. Austin focused on "how to do things with words" in developing his insights into the "performative" force of language. In addition to offering greetings, giving orders, making requests, asking questions and such, we also perform ceremonies, offer apologies, make promises, and hand out compliments. Even when we seem to be merely describing something, we make the implicit claim that this is a true description, that this is how it is with the object or situation in question. Such "speech-acts" actually constitute deeds accomplished in the world; they alter our environment and behavior.

It is by means of participating in this pragmatic dimension of linguistic activity that potential speakers are carried across the language threshold into speech. It is in this way that language serves as the primary medium through which infants are incorporated into the human-way-of-being-in-the-world. The simple learning and accomplishment of tasks can be nothing but operant conditioning, but when it is intertwined with speech, it is somehow transformed into the means of endowing potential human speakers with both speech and humanity. Unlike books, however, human language and embodiment cannot be picked up or set aside when a given task arises or is completed. Once we have indwelt our bodies and speech, they come to indwell us so as to become coextensive and synonymous with our very selves. This indwelling is accomplished by means of our participation in the pragmatic dimension of life and language.

Of course, what makes the above task-oriented processes effective is their integral relationship to the broader social contexts within which they are embedded. This brings us to the fourth major theme arising from the discussions in the previous chapters. Clearly, the specific tasks and their accompanying language patterns do not occur in a social vacuum. Rather, they are woven into the very fabric of various complex, at times overlapping and crisscrossing patterns of social interaction that Wittgenstein labeled "language-games." By imitating and learning individual behaviors and utterances that at first may be experienced as somewhat random and isolated acts, a prelinguistic being is drawn into a wider horizon of meaningful human activity. Verbally identifying and placing dishes and silverware in their respective receptacles, for instance, is a part of the larger game of "doing the dishes," which in turn finds its significance within the broad pattern known as "housekeeping." Housekeeping itself can be seen as part of the general notions of stewardship and public responsibility, and so on.

Being drawn into these increasingly rich and more comprehensive concentric circles of meaning, a potential speaker is slowly and imperceptibly transported across the threshold of language. Dogs, chimps, and human infants, for example, can all be taught to participate in certain ball games that involve minimal linguistic patterns. As the games grow in complexity, however, dogs and chimps become unable to participate at differing levels, while human infants eventually learn to participate at even higher levels. The behavioral dimension of such performance is inextricably intertwined with the linguistic dimension so as to form, together, the cognitive reality designated "learning." If the increased complexity and broadened context are progressively assimilated by the learner, then at some point he or she can be said to have become a full member of the human community. Chimpanzees and feral children both flirt with this threshold, though from opposite sides. The former seem to be capable of at least partial participation in the human community by means of sign language, while the latter seem largely to fall beneath the threshold of full humanity.

Wittgenstein grounded his notion of language-game in what he termed "forms of life." Although there is some scholarly debate over the exact meaning of this term, it seems clear that he meant to designate the human-way-of-being-in-the-world as distinguished from other natural life forms and species. While this is not the place to go into interpretive difficulties surrounding this issue, it is sufficient to suggest that the human form of life, in contrast to other natural forms, is characterized by full participation in the exceedingly rich and nuanced phenomenon of language. Although the line of demarcation between this form and others may be one of degree rather than one of the kind, it remains safe to say that this line or threshold is inextricably bound up with linguistic activity within the context of social interaction. To the degree that one can and does participate in the various language-games comprising shared intentional activity of the social level, to that degree one can be said to participate in the human form of life.

Perhaps it should go without saying that the type of cognitive dynamic involved in all of the foregoing considerations is primarily one of tacit knowing. Nevertheless, it is advisable to tarry over this, the fifth theme surfacing from the preceding investigations, since it is so fundamental. Even though a certain amount of the language instruction operative in some of the situations described in the previous chapters was explicit in nature, in the vast majority of cases the primary learning contexts were provided by informal, indirect, and implicit interactions. Moreover, the explicit teaching settings were employed only with those learners who had attained chronological or physiological age beyond that of childhood. From a logical point of view, all explicit learning requires the use of previously learned elements, since unfamiliar items must be explained in terms of familiar ones. Clearly, this explanatory chain must begin with knowledge that was not acquired explicitly; otherwise it could never get started in the first place.

The normal human child acquires language primarily through the "side door," or by "cognitive osmosis," rather than by explicit instruction. It is not possible to give a child a vocabulary list and the rules of grammar as a prerequisite to learning language. Even simple ostensive definitions presuppose a tacit grounding in a myriad of previously shared activities from within which to grasp the significance of pointing and such relative pronouns as "this," "that," "here," and "there." The grasping of explicit designations and instructions draws heavily and parasitically on a whole host of nonexplicit interactions of both a linguistic and nonlinguistic nature, such as those presented in the early pages of this concluding summation. Songs, whispers, pattycake games, overheard conversations, and imperative utterances all form the subsidiary background that provides the tacit foothold for subsequent explicit verbal instruction and learning.

Two cases in point clearly demonstrate the tacit matrix of explicit linguistic knowledge. Seated around the dinner table with other speaking members of the family, prelinguistic children will often seek to be included in the ebb and flow of the lively conversation by abruptly inserting themselves therein with outbursts of nonsense utterances and loud laughter. The children sense the interactive character of the "game" and make their contributions in what appear to them to be the same "currency." In like manner, the same children may entertain themselves for long periods of time by "talking" on toy telephones. If one listens carefully, it is easy to discern that questions are being asked, orders given, declarations made, and jokes understood, all without any vocabulary. Such "pretensions" are the seedbed from which more explicit participation in speech will spring. In such cases the children are, in Polanyi's terminology, "indwelling" linguistic activity so that later it can come to indwell them.

The mystery of the tacit character of the ground of speech, as well as of all learning, runs counter to the fundamental atomism and reductionism of the Western heritage. In assuming that all phenomena will yield to an analytic breakdown of its basic elements, we also presuppose that knowledge is composed of a quantitative accumulation of these essentially independent and isolatable conceptual units. The plain fact of both experience and logic, however, is that no one has or can isolate any such atomic building blocks. The fundamental "given" is far more holistic and organic than such a view will allow. Also, as was mentioned a bit earlier, explicit knowing logically requires a tacit ground, since otherwise an infinite regress is the result. Even contemporary subatomic physicists no longer look for the tiny indestructible particles out of which the universe is supposed to be composed. These scientists now prefer to speak of the "stuff" of nature as organized patterns of energy in motion, finding little or no use of the notion of "matter" at all.

The linguistic parallel to these epistemological and metaphysical reflections brings us to a sixth motif arising from the investigations of the previous chapters, namely, the cruciality of the metaphoric mode. The assumption that language ultimately must break down into independent units of meaning that designate isolatable entities and qualities of reality has pervaded the entire history of Western thought.

Beginning with Plato's theory of Forms right down to Bertrand Russell's "logical atomism," it has been presupposed that unequivocal meaning and absolute precision must be both the basis of all language and the goal of all comprehension. The mature work of Ludwig Wittgenstein has served as the fulcrum for dismantling this "luggage tag" or "picture theory" of meaning. Use and context are now seen as the primary bearers of meaning, and significant precision has come to serve as its standard of success. Communication is now understood as far more diverse, organic, and flexible than any univocal atomism could allow. This revolution has opened the way to a far more fruitful appreciation of the crucial role of metaphor in human speech.

In the traditional view of communication, literal significance is taken to be the basis out of which figurative or metaphorical significance might arise. Although this view seems to explain a good deal at the surface level of language, as with most poetry of the "rosy fingers of dawn" variety, it will not hold up as an account of how language works at the more primary level. First, it is logically impossible to begin language with literal or precise meanings because such meanings presuppose previous ones by means of which these are identified or crafted. Even the terms "literal," "precise," and "metaphor" are, along with the vast majority of so-called literal speech, themselves "dead" metaphors. There once was a *New Yorker* cartoon that forcefully illustrates this important point. In it one caveman says to another: "Now that we have invented language, let us not engage in any vague generalities."

Owen Barfield has made this same point in a most interesting manner. He calls attention to the strange contradiction between the received view of the historical development of language and our traditional view of the logical nature of language. According to the former, ancient peoples spoke and lived within the metaphoric mode by means of their mythologies and archaic symbols, while modern peoples have replaced this mode with the precision of science and logic. According to the latter, literal language is logically prior to the metaphoric mode, so it clearly must antedate it. Obviously, both cannot be true. Barfield argues cogently that both historically and conceptually the symbiotic relation between language and reality must precede the separation between them that has characterized the Western view at least since the early Greek philosophers. This symbiosis is the very heart of the metaphoric mode of communication, which, as Aristotle (who was generally ahead of his time) put it, "is the greatest thing by far since it is the true sign of genius."

All of this is well borne out by the various studies examined in this present book. To the degree that every case of communication depends heavily upon what Austin called the "illocutionary force" of an utterance, together with an understanding of the social and physical context, to that degree it embodies aspects of metaphor. Everyone who communicates, whether with normal children, chimpanzees, feral or autistic children, or people of another culture, must draw upon such factors in order to create a range of meaning within which to accomplish the given task. Even within this range of meaning, what is attained is a degree of precision sufficient or appropriate to a given situation. Thus in each case one communicates against a broad background of ambiguity and vagueness, the horizon of which is only drawn as tight as is necessary to accomplish one's purposes. This "cinching up" of ambiguity and vagueness is accomplished by first establishing initial metaphorical connections and then parsing off more specific meanings as the occasions arise.

When my youngest son was but a few months old, I used to go into his room every morning and ask if he wanted to get "up." As I looked down at him in the crib, I would ask repeatedly "up?" The background and intentional significance of this utterance was obviously vague or ambiguous at the outset. The morning sun, my smiling face, the sounds of the words, the sensation of being lifted out of the crib, of being hugged were all an integral part of the meaning for him. Moreover, these various phenomena were not independent and distinguishable factors comprising this situation for him, but together they were its meaning. Slowly, through the push-and-pull of our daily life together, he began to sort out various aspects from one another and associate them with different, more specific locutions. At the outset, however, "up" was characterized by the poly-significance inherent within the metaphoric mode.

It is this deep, primal quality of metaphor that both makes possible and accounts for the delight in the spontaneous connections expressed in the linguistic innovations offered by those who live on the threshold of language. The chimps and feral children, no less than normal human children and those learning a second language, all give evidence at least occasionally of participating in this metaphoric mode. As I have mentioned, my own son, when but sixteen months old, expressed the isomorphism that he recognized between an apple and a basketball in the form of a joke when he pretended to take a bite out of the basketball and asked with a wide smile, "Apple?"

In the process of reviewing and reflecting on the particulars, as well as on the thematic dynamics, of the investigations here under discussion, the focal image that suggests itself most forcefully is that of the dance. In every case and at all levels, prelinguistic beings are, in a very real sense, invited by the members of the speaking community to participate in a social activity that is already in process and ongoing. At the same time, however, it must be noted that this "invitation" is not of a formal nature; it is more a matter of being caught up in a swirling group activity without ever really being asked. As existentialist thinkers characterize our existence as that of having been "thrown" into life, so our linguisticality is that of having been "swept away" by language.

Without knowing the steps, indeed, without even being aware that there are steps, the prelinguistic being is taken by the hands and drawn into the speaking community as it whirls around in the space and among the furniture provided by the natural environment. Although the steps are extremely complex, one's immediate dancing partners frequently separate themselves from the larger circle in order to provide slowed-down and simplified instruction. Slowly one gets the hang of some of the steps, finds one's feet, as it were, and is simply dragged along by the larger group for the rest. It is an immensely frustrating yet exhilarating experience; the expectations of the other, adult dancers are so demanding, yet the rewards of participation are so enriching.

Perhaps the most interesting yet perplexing aspect of the dance of language is the fact that there are so many "dances within dances," so many spinoff groups engaged in specialized routines even while continuing to participate in the larger, overall dance. Over here, for example, is a circle of dancers doing a kind of two-step in a side-by-side alignment while still moving to the same rhythm as the larger group encircling them with a skip-step. Over there a group has broken off into waltzing couples, while the dancers at the center are spinning in a circle dance. The most amazing thing is that not only do these various groups weave in and out of one another, frequently metamorphosing and merging into other formations, but both the steps and the individual dancers are continuously altered and exchanged. Although there are occasional confusions and falterings, resulting in both breakdowns and innovation, for the most part these are somehow absorbed into the dominant ebb and flow of the larger dance or dances.

Of course, some folks turn out to be better dancers than others, at least with respect to a given step or circle of dancers. And some do not seem to be able to get the hang of it at all, or only partially. These turn out to be the interesting cases with regard to locating and sketching the contours of the language threshold. Sometimes it is difficult to determine whether or not a particular dancer or group is in fact dancing at all. Perhaps they are imitating certain simple steps and routines but cannot actually go on to more complex patterns or develop any steps of their own. On the other hand, perhaps their particular version of movement can or will be incorporated into the broader dance pattern, forcing us to redefine our notion of the threshold or of dancing itself!

It seems clear that the notion of threshold, when applied to an activity, functions differently from how it is thought of in a spatial context. In the latter, it can in theory always be determined whether or not one has crossed a given threshold. All that is necessary is to establish an agreed-upon line of demarcation. In the present case, however, the definition of what constitutes actually speaking a language, actually dancing rather than merely jumping around, is itself in constant flux and subject to ongoing interpretation. Thus the threshold of language, like that of dancing, is largely a function of the interaction among those whose participation constitutes the activity itself.

In my mind, or better yet, in my mind-body, this image of the dance forcefully focuses the many diverse dimensions of the language phenomenon. The axial role of the body, the reciprocity among speaking agents, the specifics of task orientation, the social and contextual variations, the primacy of tacit knowing, and the freedom of meta-phorical extension are all exhibited in the complexities and progressions of dancing. Perhaps this image can be put to fruitful use in further investigation and reflections on the mysterious yet all-pervasive character of language, for those of us seeking to understand this many-splendored phenomenon are still only at its threshold.

A "Concluding Unscientific Postscript"

Borrowing from the title of one of Søren Kierkegaard's most important works, I would like to finish up by offering a brief response to Steven Pinker's recent and popular book, *The Language Instinct*. Pinker distinguishes his own approach to language acquisition from that of both psycholinguistics and Noam Chomsky by insisting on the biological and evolutionary basis of language. As he puts it:

> Language is not a cultural artifact that we learn the way we learn to tell time or how the federal government works. Instead, it is a distinct piece of the biological makeup of our brains. Language is a complex, specialized skill, which develops in the child spontaneously, without conscious effort or formal instruction . . . some cognitive scientists have described language as a psychological faculty, a mental organ, a neural system, and a computation module. But I prefer the admittedly quaint term "instinct." It conveys the idea that people know how to talk in more or less the same sense that spiders know how to spin webs. (p. 18)

In my opinion, the clarity and informative quality of Pinker's book are nearly canceled out by the breezy manner in which he dismisses views of language acquisition that do not conform to his own view and by the limited scope of his "positivist" understanding of science. Moreover, he has an annoying habit of moving through his line of argument by using "maybe," "perhaps," and "it could be the case," but ending up with resounding conclusions that are "inescapable." The real problem with Pinker's approach, however, is to be found within the concept of "instinct" itself.

The difficulty with claiming that language acquisition is a function of instinct revolves around the simple fact that instinctive behavior is generally understood as exhibiting itself even in the absence of external input from or interaction with the "social" environment. To use Pinker's example of the spider, the astonishing difference between spiders' web spinning and children's speech is that the spider will spin webs whether or not it has ever seen another spider do so. The spider's instinct is in no way dependent on interaction with other spiders. But the very opposite is true of children with respect to speech; without some form of linguistic community and activity, children will simply not speak at all. Thus it is misleading at best and downright question begging at worst to claim that language acquisition is essentially instinctive.

Another way to put this objection is in terms of evolution itself. Pinker is at pains to explain how various instincts can be understood as the exclusive result of natural selection, which operates in relation to alterations in the environment. This works quite well when the relevant environment is strictly physical in nature, since such an environment is already present when the organism arrives on the scene. It exists independent of the organism, and purely physical skills can arise through interaction with it. This cannot be the case with language, however, since to posit the prior existence of a linguistic environment presupposes the very phenomenon that is supposedly being explained. Thus in a very real sense, speech must be acquired from speakers.

Having explained the initial advent of the language instinct in terms of genetic mutation, Pinker faces the problem of explaining to whom the first being so programmed would have spoken. His answer to this crucial question turns out to be little more than a vague conjecture about others being able to at least partially understand "what the mutant was saying even if they lacked the new-fangled circuitry, just using overall intelligence" (p. 365). Thus Pinker clearly has people speaking before there are other speakers and/or hearers. But the evidence is clear that without a speaking environment children simply do not speak at all. Their prelinguistic oral play must be engaged, stimulated, and expected if they are to become members of the speaking community. If this is true of children today, it certainly would have been true of any genetic mutant eons ago. Since the linguistic environment necessary to the natural selection of language was by definition absent, a strictly evolutionary explanation of speech leaves a great deal yet to be explained.

Although it is clear that the circuitry of the brain must play a crucial role in any explanation of language acquisition, it is equally clear that somatic and social interaction are required in the learning of this most amazing and mysterious of human skills. The overwhelming convergence of the cases examined in the preceding chapters on these two factors as central to the acquisition of speech should be sufficient cause for embarking on a much broader, multidimensional exploration than has thus far been envisioned by those interested in this phenomenon.

Bibliography

Austin, J. *How to Do Things with Words*. Cambridge, Mass.: Harvard University Press, 1962.

Barfield, O. *Poetic Diction*. Middletown, Conn.: Wesleyan University Press, 1973.

Berkeley, G. *Principles of Human Knowledge*. Any edition.

Bettelheim, B. "Feral Children and Autistic Children," *American Journal of Sociology* 64 (1969), pp. 455–67.

Bloom, P. *Language Acquisition*. Cambridge, Mass.: MIT Press, 1994.

Cassirer, E. *The Philosophy of Symbolic Forms*. New Haven, Conn.: Yale University Press, 1957.

Chomsky, N. *Reflections on Language*. New York: Random House, 1975.

Gadamer, H-G. *Philosophical Hermeneutics*. Berkeley: University of California Press, 1976.

Gardner, R., and B. Gardner. *Teaching Sign Language to Chimpanzees*. Albany: SUNY Press, 1989.

Gesell, A. *Wolf Child and Human Child*. London: Methuen, 1941.

Goodman, N. *Ways of Worldmaking*. Indianapolis: Hackett Publishers, 1978.

Kant, I. *Critique of Pure Reason*. Any edition.

Kaufman, B., and S. Kaufman. *Son Rise: The Miracle Continues*. Tiburon, Cal.: Kramer, 1994.

Keller, H. *The Story of My Life*. New York: Doubleday, 1903.

———. *Teacher*. Garden City, N.Y.: Doubleday, 1955.

Kuhn, T. *The Structure of Scientific Revolutions*. Chicago: University of Chicago Press, 1970.

Lakoff, G., and Johnson, M. *Metaphors We Live By*. Chicago: University of Chicago Press, 1980.

Lee, L. "Some Semantic Goals for Aphasia Therapy," *ETC*, vol. 18, no. 3 (1963).

Locke, J. *Essay Concerning Human Understanding*. Any edition.

Malson, L. *Wolf Children and the Problem of Human Nature*. New York: Monthly Review Press, 1972.

Mead, G. H. *On Social Psychology*. Chicago: University of Chicago Press, 1952.

Merleau-Ponty, M. *Phenomenology of Perception*. New York: Humanities Press, 1962.

Murray, D. *Forked Tongues: Speech, Writing, and Representation in North American Indian Texts*. London: Pinter Press, 1991.

Percy, W. *The Message in the Bottle*. New York: Farrar, Straus and Giroux, 1976.

Piaget, J. *Six Psychological Studies*. New York: Random House, 1967.

Pinker, S. *The Language Instinct*. New York: HarperCollins, 1994.

Plato. *The Sophist.* Any edition.

Polanyi, M. *Personal Knowledge.* New York, Harper & Row, 1958.

Rogers, L. "Hemisphere Specialization in Language," Paper presented at Conference on Human Brain Function, UCLA Brain Institute, 1976.

Skinner, B. F. *Verbal Behavior.* Cambridge, Mass.: MIT Press, 1957.

Taylor, E. "Wild Men and Beast Children." *Anthropological Review* 1 (1863), 21–32.

Whorf, B. *Language, Thought, and Reality.* Edited by John B. Carroll. Cambridge, Mass.: MIT Press, 1956.

Wittgenstein, L. *Philosophical Investigations.* New York: Macmillan, 1953.

———. *Tractatus Logico-Philosophicus.* New York: Humanities Press, 1961.

Zingg, R. M. "Feral Men and Extreme Cases of Isolation." *American Journal of Psychology* 53 (1940), 487–517.

Index

ABOUT THE AUTHOR

Jerry H. Gill has authored nine books, edited
five books, and published more than one hundred
journal articles on the philosophy of language, epistemology, Native American religions, ethics, and
theology. Previously he was a professor of philosophy
and religious studies at the College of Saint Rose in
Albany, New York, and was on the faculty of Eckerd
College in St. Petersburg, Florida. Professor Gill
now teaches at Pima Community College in Tucson,
Arizona, where he is writing a book about Native
American worldviews. He likes to hike, sculpt, and
play basketball, and especially enjoys travel to
Greece and Finland, the homeland of his wife and
colleague, Mari Sorri.